# Great Possibilities for your home

A Bantam Book / published in association with
Hudson Publishing / May 1979
for Georgia-Pacific Corporation

For information write: Georgia-Pacific Corporation, 900 S.W. Fifth Avenue, Portland, OR 97204

Executive Editor: Robert J. Dunn
Project Design / Writing: R.J. De Cristoforo
Project Design / Illustrations: Kenneth Vendley
Art Director: Burt Sakai
Editors: Cheryl Nafzgar, Sally Harms
Layout Design: Joan Brown
Production: Laurie Blackman

Printed in the United States of America

Library of Congress catalog number: 79-51186

ISBN: 0-553-19130-6

**Georgia-Pacific will not be responsible for any illness, injury, damages, claims, suits, actions, or loss of any kind whatsoever or however caused arising from the use or misuse of the information and/or drawings contained herein.**

Black and white text: Georgia-Pacific's Econoprint Offset 50 lb.
Four Color Section: Georgia-Pacific's Mall City Matte 50 lb.

# CONTENTS

## WOOD . . . Mother Nature's Renewable Resource

Helping Mother Nature do a better job is one of the major goals of Georgia-Pacific foresters. The company operates on over 6.5 million acres of timberlands scientifically managed under a sustained growth program.

To provide a never-ending supply of timber and wood for its customers, Georgia-Pacific foresters manage 16 seed orchards and five nurseries in the U.S. and one in Canada. These nurseries have the capacity to grow 19 million super seedlings annually. Millions of these seedlings, from scientifically controlled parent stock, can grow to marketable size in half the time usually required by Mother Nature unaided.

Georgia-Pacific tries to get maximum yield from the harvests. Practically all of each log is utilized. In addition, the company annually recycles millions of tons of manufacturing residue and solid waste . . . newspapers, magazines, corrugated boxes, wood chips, sawdust, fines, slabs, chunks, and plywood peeler cores . . . all manufactured into useful products.

Over 42 percent of the company's energy needs are generated internally by Georgia-Pacific from waste, such as tree bark, to help solve energy problems.

# ABOUT THIS BOOK

This book offers you, the reader, a combination of exciting new ideas, project plans, and how-to-do-it information that will help you take advantage of the many GREAT POSSIBILITIES to make your home a better place to live. The ideas should be the foundation for other improvements you have in mind for your living environment. Familiarize yourself with our *modus operandi*, as this will help you understand the individual projects even more. Any project, no matter how big or small, should be well planned. Take the time to consider what your results will be. Make sure the project blends well with the rest of your home environment. It's most important also that you schedule your project time carefully so that it doesn't drag on. Finally, if you carefully analyze the ideas and projects published here, you'll be able to pick those that best reflect the GREAT POSSIBILITIES for your home.

We are presenting to you as you embark on the exciting journey of home improvement the opportunity to do major structural remodeling, build furniture and small structures, and make decorative improvements on your home. **Chapter 1, Gaining Valuable Space**, is the section to turn to first if your home no longer meets the space needs of your family. We provide the inspirational ideas and basic outlines that allow the experienced home handyperson to proceed on the remodeling project of his choice.

No previous experience at all is required for the projects in **Chapter 2, Easy-to-Build Projects (with plans included)**. We provide step-by-step instructions and easy-to-follow technical drawings that will enable you to create lovely pieces of furniture like the Coffee Table Plus Seats pictured here.

For more ambitious projects you need go no further than our **Chapter 3, Great Home Improvement Possibilities (with plans you can buy).** It would demand too much space for a book this size to include the plans for these projects, so we have provided you with an order blank on page 207 so you can purchase them by mail. The end result can be something as beautiful as this Bay Window—Window Garden.

**Chapter 4, How to Create Decorative Elegance**, is the place to look for major redecorating projects. Although they don't involve major structural changes, these projects can add untold elegance to your home, as you can see from this rendering of How to Add Ceiling Beams.

**Chapter 5, Basic Tools and Product Data**, tells how to shop for the tools and materials you'll need for your projects. If you are a first-time do-it-yourselfer, your helpful Georgia-Pacific Registered Building Materials Dealer will be glad to answer any questions you might have. Be sure to ask about his Redi-Cut plywood, lumber, hardboard, and particleboard pieces that are precut and more convenient to use. These precut materials can save you time and dollars in your project planning.

We know you'll be inspired by our sixteen pages of colorful ideas using Georgia-Pacific products to create these good-looking effects. Your G-P dealer has a full line of samples and literature to help you achieve the same beauty in your home.

# 1/ GAINING VALUABLE SPACE

The need for additional space — for a variety of reasons — is a common plight among homeowners. This is particularly true now with the price of housing soaring as it is. In the not-too-distant past, it was a relatively simple process to sell a home and invest in a larger one as space needs increased. Nowadays, more and more families are discovering the wisdom of staying put and creating new spaces in, on, above, and adjacent to their current home. They are, in effect, creating a new home at the old address. In this first chapter, we're presenting a variety of ideas that you can adapt to your personal space needs . . . and we've added some technical drawings to help you visualize some of the more difficult aspects of each project. Adopt an idea and execute it well. You'll have more space and, happily, you will have added more dollar value to your home.

# BUILD OUT FOR MORE LIVING SPACE

It was normal at one time for a family to seek a larger house when it outgrew what it had. The same solution may not be so desirable today. Inflated prices can make the house-sale profit seem negligible — inadequate for swinging the new deal. An answer? Expansion possibilities that exist in the present home. It is rare for a lot size to be so small that it can't accommodate an additional room, or two.

The first step is to check local codes and zoning laws. They will say where you can build and how close to property lines you can come. There will be restrictions, and it's best to know right away what they are.

Second step — not absolutely necessary but wise — engage an architect who will work with you to design the addition and who will produce plans you can submit to building inspectors without blushing.

Primary considerations must be how the room will be used. In a bedroom, electrical factors will be minor. In a bathroom, plumbing becomes critical. How will the room be heated? You can do it simply with electric panel or baseboard heaters, or you can extend the existing system. Maybe a fireplace will do; prefab, recirculating types are a smart way to go today and quite easy to install. The foundation? Will it be concrete slab or a crawl-space type?

If you are knowledgeable enough or care to do enough research, you can provide the answers and even produce respectable drawings; but the expertise of a professional can make short work of getting to the point when you start building.

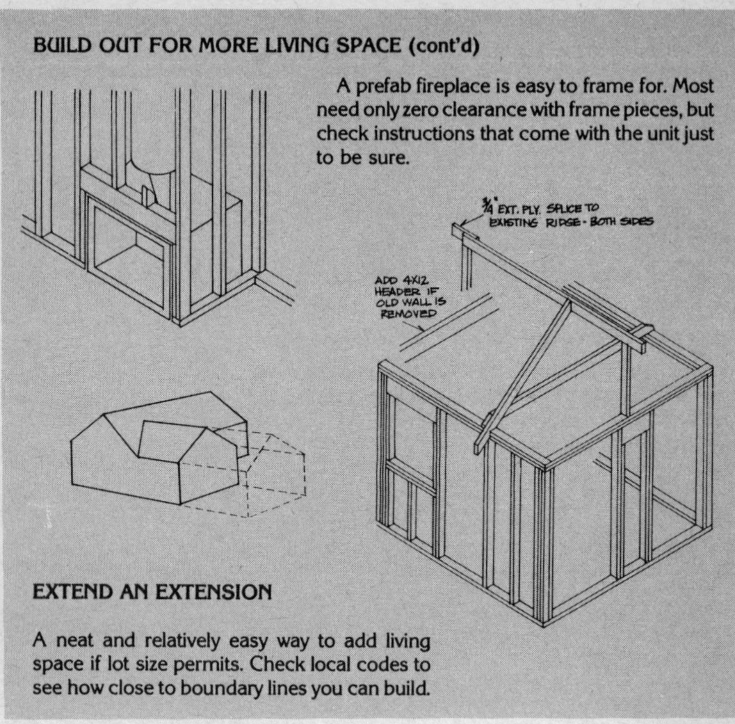


**BUILD OUT FOR MORE LIVING SPACE (cont'd)**

A prefab fireplace is easy to frame for. Most need only zero clearance with frame pieces, but check instructions that come with the unit just to be sure.

**EXTEND AN EXTENSION**

A neat and relatively easy way to add living space if lot size permits. Check local codes to see how close to boundary lines you can build.

The big question: how much of the physical work will you do? It's not uncommon for the lay-person to do everything, thereby saving a considerable amount in labor costs; but a less exhausting method — once you are armed with the important building permit — is to become a homeowner/contractor. You decide what you want done and what you will do yourself.

Frequently, the homeowner will have professionals carry the job up to the point of inside and outside finishing. Covering the frame with modern materials is the interesting part of the job anyway. Here, you may be restricted to existing siding materials on the house if you wish the addition to blend exactly. Inside finishing is something else. You can choose from the many materials available: gypsum wallboard, paint, wallpaper, plywood paneling, lumber, or plywood siding. This is a way to do an attractive project in an exclusive way.

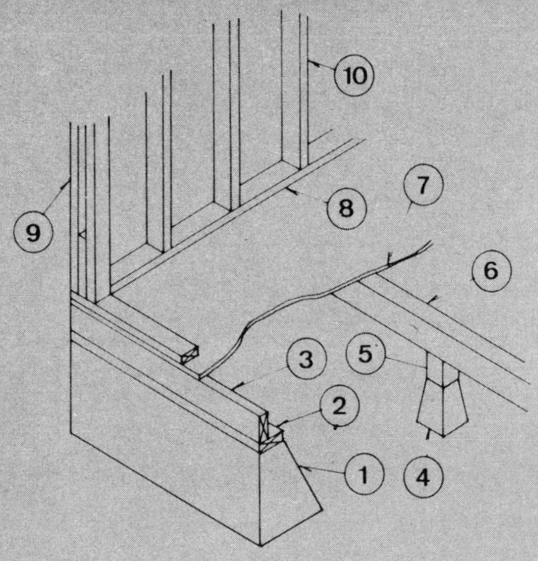


**A QUICK FLOOR OVER A CRAWL SPACE**

1 perimeter foundation walls
2 2x6 sill (treated)
3 2x6 stringer or "band"
4 precast concrete piers set on small concrete base
5 4x4 post (treated)
6 joists — 2x lumber at 32" on centers or 4x beams at 48" on centers
7 Special 1⅛" plywood with tongue-and-groove edges serves as both subfloor and underlayment. Finish floor — resilient tile, carpeting, linoleum, may be laid directly.
8 sole plate
9 corner post assembly
10 studs

# CAN'T BUILD OUT? MAYBE UP!

Building up is a feasible way to add more living space, and it can be less of a chore than building out. For one thing, you don't have to provide a foundation! Of course the strength of the existing structure should be checked either by a professional you hire or by local authorities who, finally, will be the ones to say whether you can or can't build where you want. Since most houses are structurally capable of supporting a second story, getting a permit shouldn't be a problem. Many additions of this nature are done over a garage since it's usually an area that permits the work with the least amount of structural change.

Overall, the job consists of removing roof components and then erecting the framework of the addition over the existing walls. Whatever strengthening of the walls that might be required should be done before the new work is started. Relocate existing joists so they fall into the 16″ on-center pattern of the joists you add for the new floor. Some projection beyond the perimeter wall (a small balcony or a bay window?) may be permitted. If so, now is the time to provide joist support.

## CAN'T BUILD OUT? MAYBE UP! (cont'd)

When the projection is in line with the run of the joists, it may be possible to use longer joists and cantilever them as shown.

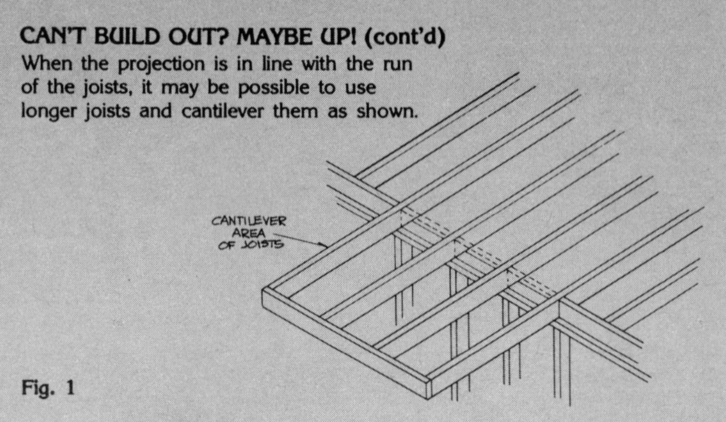


Fig. 1

Regular joists can be extended; cantilever joists that parallel regular joists can be organized as shown in the drawing (see Fig. 1). A general rule says that the distance from the wall to the doubled joist should be twice the length of the overhang.

Also, now is the time to consider any openings through the floor — a stairway? See the drawing (Fig. 2) for the special arrangement that is required to supply strength lost when joists are cut. If a stairway is necessary, but you don't wish to lose inside room, consider one built outside.

Flooring can be done with a subfloor over which you place an underlayment as the base for the finish floor or by using special plywood panels (as thick as 1⅛" and as large as 4' x 12') — structural elements to which you can apply a finish floor directly (see Fig. 3).

Framing is next: treated sole plate, studs, rafter plates, and so on. This part of the job goes quickly. Adding inside and outside wall coverings takes more time, but that's okay since it's the more pleasant part of the operation. Be selective. Carefully check all the modern materials that offer so many options. Gypsum wallboard, prefinished plywoods and hardboards — many of them available with harmonizing mouldings that make professional installations easy to do — are fine for the inside. Lumber, plywood, and hardboard sidings with various surface textures and patterns are good for the outside. Most lumber yards have such materials on display.

Incidentally, don't neglect insulation in the floor, the walls and over the new ceiling. Insulation can be blanket or batt (made of fiberglass, cotton, wood fiber, or mineral wool), loose-fill insulation (made of vermiculite, mineral wool, or cellulose), blown insulation (made of urea formaldehyde or loose-fill material), foamboard or fiberboard sheathing. Making a snug room is easy now before framing is covered.

An opening through floor framing (for a stairway?) must be organized to compensate for strength lost when regular joists are cut. This design is common.

1 Outline joists are doubled (called trimmers).
2 Doubled "header" joists are added.
3 The cut joists are called "tail" joists.

*Note* . . . . spacing of regular joists should be consistent. When necessary, trimmer joists should be included as *additional* pieces.

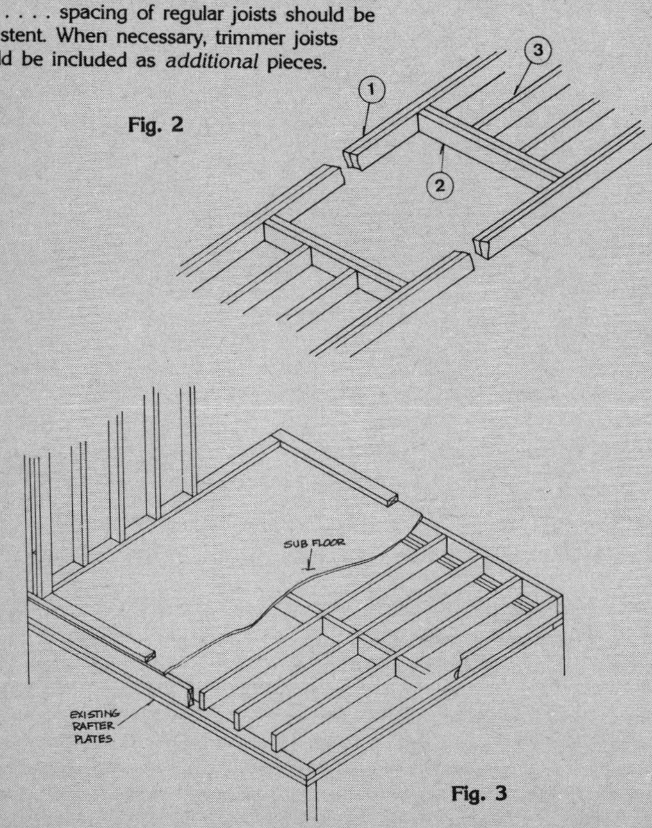


**Fig. 2**

**Fig. 3**

before

# REMOVE A WALL FOR AN OPEN PLAN

This is a good way to convert two small rooms to one spacious one. To begin with, determine whether the wall is "bearing" or "nonbearing." As the name implies, the bearing wall carries the weight of what is above. When one is removed, a substitute support — usually a 4x12 beam — must be installed in its place. A nonbearing wall can be removed without fear of weakening the structure.

All outside walls are bearing walls. To judge partitions, determine their directional relationship to the ceiling joists. A partition that is parallel to joists is nonbearing. One that runs at right angles to joists is carrying weight and is structurally critical. Actually any partition, especially in older homes that have settled considerably, is carrying weight. So, as is often done, a 4x12 beam is included in the remodeling no matter what. It's a safety factor, and it's decorative.

Be aware the wall may contain items that must be rerouted; you don't just cut through it. Best bet is to remove the covering on one side so you can

after

visually check, and then, if necessary, determine how best to change the course of wires and, maybe, pipes. After these jobs are done (with safety precautions like switching off electric circuits and closing the valve at the water entry), remove the second wall covering.

If you are working on a bearing wall, use temporary 2x4 braces, placed at a slight angle between the top plates and the floor to provide support while you remove the framing.

The new beam can rest on 4x4 posts that will be hidden in the side walls or on 4x6 or 4x8 beams that will project into the room. Work will be considerably reduced if you feel that a wide opening will do as well as a complete wall removal. The drawing for this concept shows how the framing is organized. If the wall is nonbearing, and if you wish, doubled 2x4s with cripple studs above can be substituted for the header.

Finishing can consist of matching sidewalls and ceiling to the old wall finishes, but a better idea is to create a completely different look by covering all walls with a decorative wall paneling.

## WHAT THE WALL FRAMING WILL LOOK LIKE

A Solid wall (no doors) will be all studs and, possibly, fire blocking.

B An opening for a door may be framed this way. Such a design usually indicates a nonbearing wall.

C Opening framed this way (with a 4x12 header) tells of a bearing wall.

D Older homes (also some new ones) may have openings framed this way (doubled 2x6 or 2x8 header) — also a sign of a bearing wall.

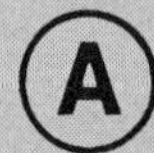

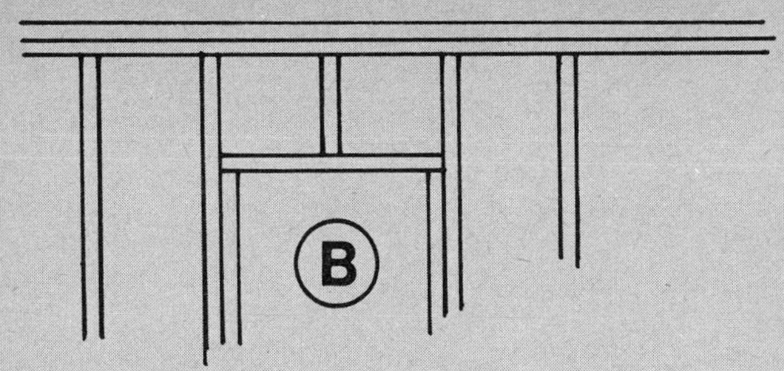
B

C

D

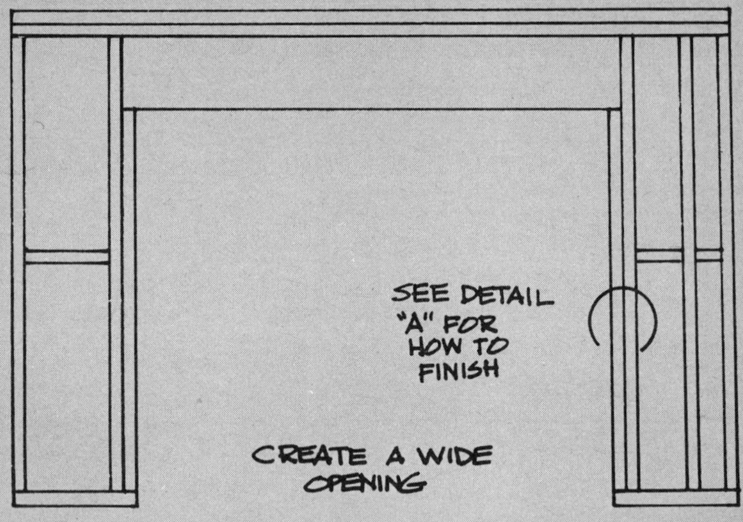


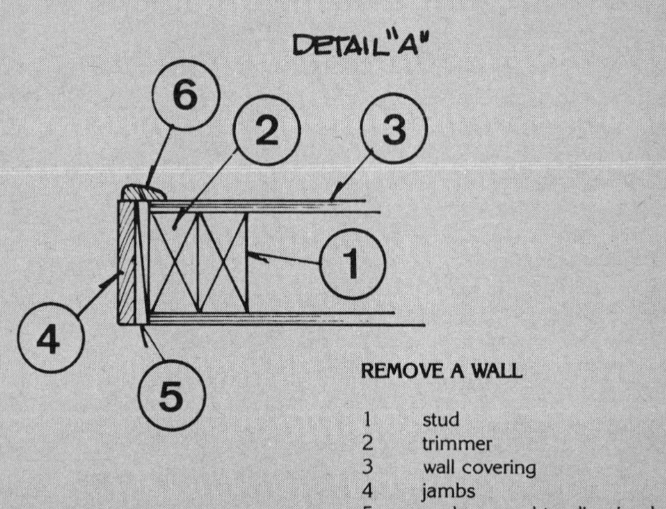


REMOVE A WALL

1 stud
2 trimmer
3 wall covering
4 jambs
5 wedges used to align jambs (usually pieces of shingling)
6 casing (moulding)

A  A 4″ beam — structural and decorative — it supports in place of the old wall. Rest it on 4x4s hidden in the side walls.
B  Use a wider post — let it project into the room.
C  Add a decorative corbel.
D  Add extra posts — install wrought iron railing between them.

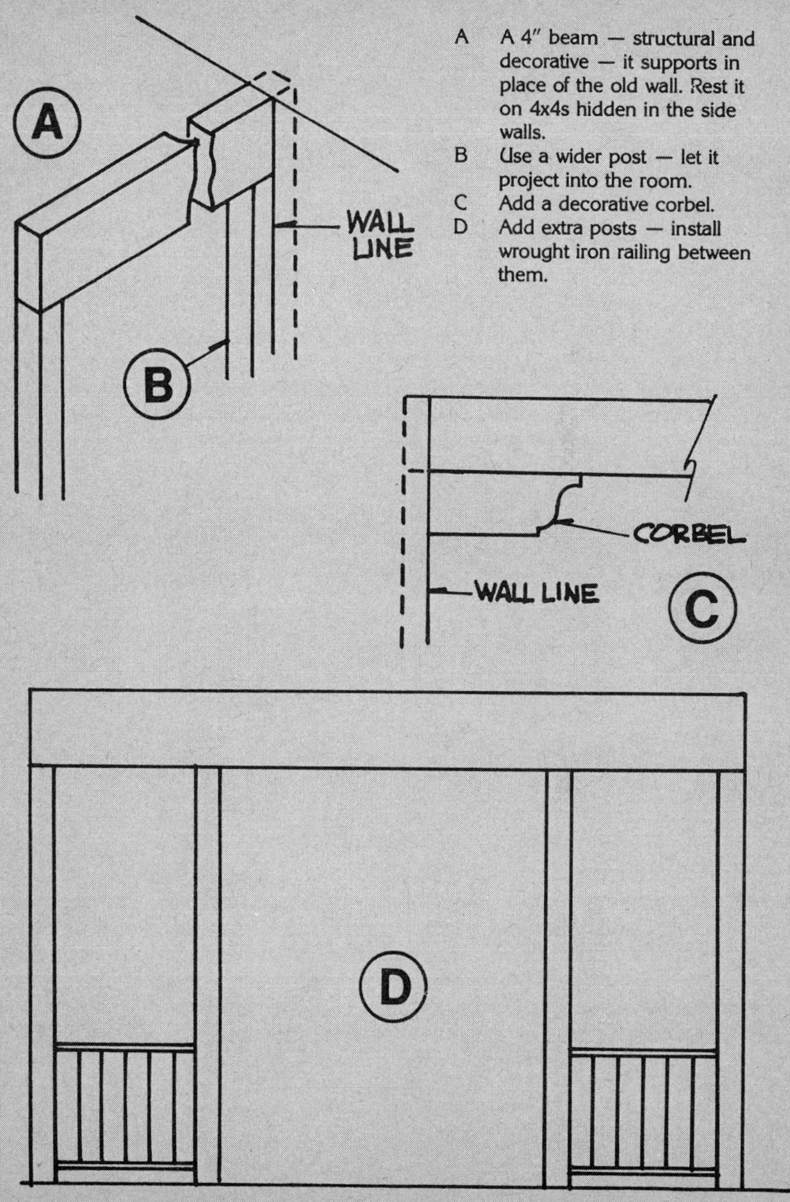

# EVICT THE CAR FOR MORE LIVING SPACE

You can't build up or out, and you wish to provide more living space with a minimum of structural work? Think of the garage. It's a readymade room that requires only closing in a wall, adding insulation, and dressing up the interior. Since the garage will already have a substantial header, the closing in will consist mostly of laying a sole plate and then erecting studs. Window openings, if any, will *not* require individual headers.

If the slab is sound and cleanable, you can lay a floor directly on the concrete by using vinyl tiles or wood block flooring that is made specifically for such an application. If the slab requires waterproofing or if you wish to have a more conventional type floor, you can use one of the three systems shown in the drawings. Do be aware that thin strip flooring will not be adequately supported by sleepers. Strips at least ¾″ thick should be considered. System three allows a conventional approach: subflooring, underlayment, and then finish floor, or, alternately, a 1⅛″ thick plywood base for direct application of finish floor.

Inside walls and the ceiling can be done with gypsum wallboard or one of the easy-to-install 4x8 decorative plywood wall panelings. Be sure that electrical wiring and any other in-the-wall elements that might be needed have been correctly installed before doing the cover-ups — and don't neglect insulation.

Feel bad about evicting the car? Provide a special home for it by adding a carport — adequate protection in most parts of the country. See page 28.

## EVICT THE CAR FOR MORE LIVING SPACE (cont'd)

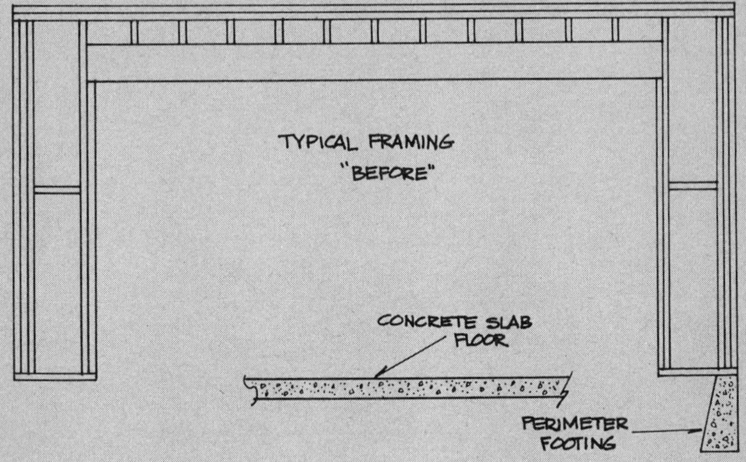


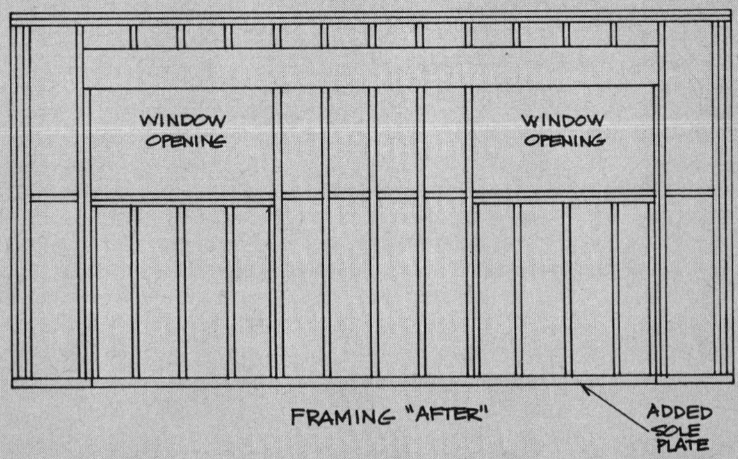


**NOTE: only treated lumber should be used when in direct contact with concrete floors.**

# FLOOR SYSTEMS

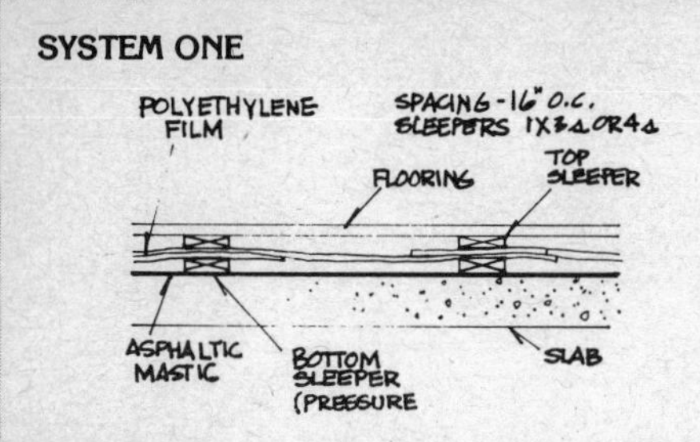


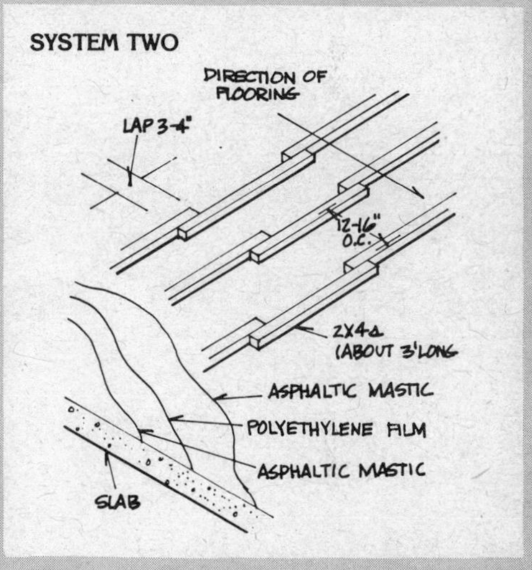


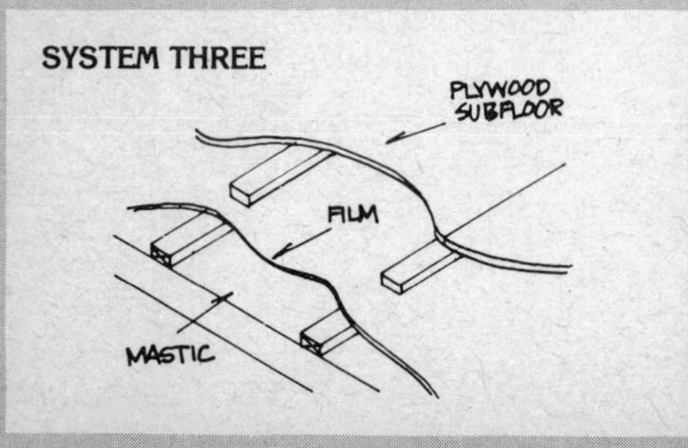

# A NEW HOME FOR THE CAR

A carport is the next project after the garage has been converted to an attractive living space, for example, or a good-size workshop. Often the carport is situated in front of the garage, its cover merely an extension of existing roof lines. This makes it possible to use the in-place driveway. If this isn't feasible, a frequent solution is erecting a shed-type structure against a wall of the house.

Either way, construction procedures can be minimized by viewing the carport as a husky frame that is there to support a roof. The drawings show the basic elements of a carport with a gable roof and one with a shed roof. In each case, heavy beams are supported by 4x4 posts, so long distances can be spanned without needing intermediate support.

The job can be done without pouring a slab — a thick bed of well-tamped gravel which can also be a lead-in from the driveway. If so, the posts must be supported with adequate concrete footings. The advantages of a slab are obvious — easy maintenance and a good floor for occasional use as a ping pong court, etc.

Sidewalls of carports are often wholly or partially closed in with simple cabinetry done with exterior grades of plywood. Thus the project can provide storage space as well as car protection.

## CARPORT WITH GABLE ROOF

1 new concrete slab
2 4x4 posts
3 4x12 beams
4 Post anchors — some made for installation when concrete is poured. Others may be added after concrete sets.
5 Heavy metal angles — use screws or bolts as fasteners.
6 beam hangers
7 Support for new ridge — spike to studs of existing wall or use beam hanger.
8 Plywood roof sheathing is base for finish roofing.
9 shingles

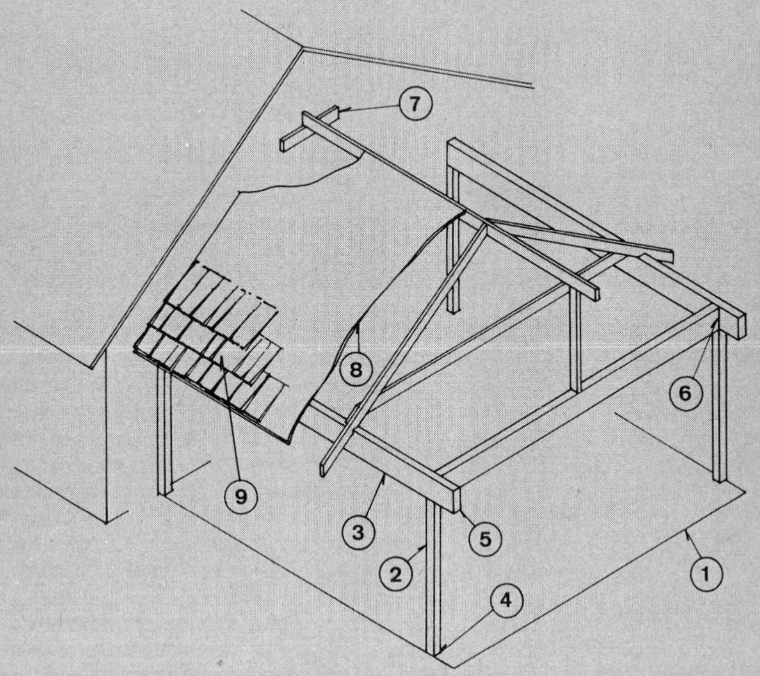

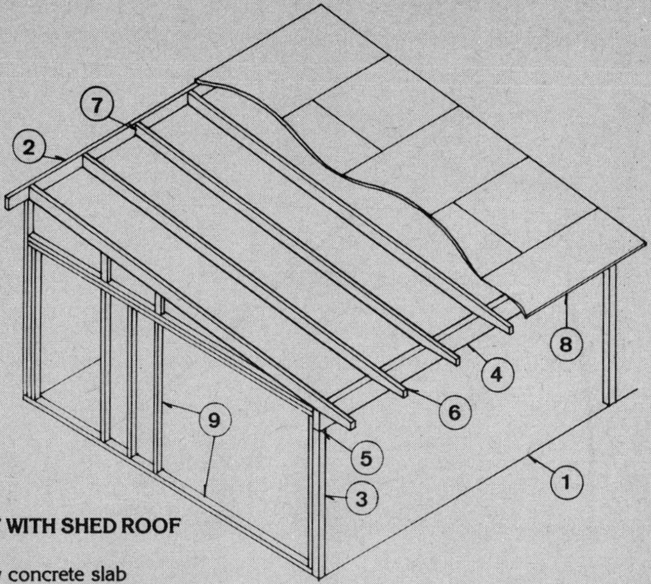

**CARPORT WITH SHED ROOF**

1 new concrete slab
2 2x6 ledger spiked or lag-screwed to studs of house wall
3 4x4 posts
4 4x12 header beam
5 post cap (readymade connector)
6 2x6 joist/rafters
7 joist hangers
8 Plywood roof sheathing to support finish roofing.
9 Optional — standard framing to fill in sides. Treated sole plate attached with case-hardened nails or with anchor bolts that were set in place when the concrete was poured.

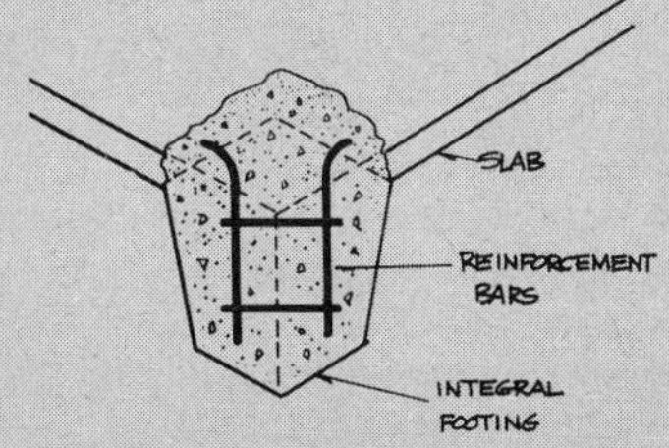


**SLAB WITH INTEGRAL FOOTINGS UNDER POST AREAS**

# REDO A BASEMENT

It's like building down, but most of the work has been done. The job consists of giving it a finished look like the rest of the house. Since most basements are rather large, some preliminary paper work is in order. How will the room be used? Full size as a playroom? Divided into specific areas for utility room, workshop? How about a wet bar, a small gym, a wine cellar? Built-ins for storage might be important. There *are* options. Make necessary decisions before the work starts.

The first step is to waterproof the area. Hydraulic cement can be used to plug joints and cracks; cementitious paint in a batter-like consistency can cover walls. The joint between wall and floor may be a special problem, but you can handle it with a heavy bead of waterproof cement. If water seepage is a severe problem, check outside. Be sure the grade slopes away from the house and that downspouts have well directed lead-offs. If necessary, dig around the wall. Seal the *outside* with a membrane waterproofing material. Once the water battle is won, you can start the fun work.

Special anchor nails (or bolts) are available for attachment of furring strips directly to concrete or concrete block walls.

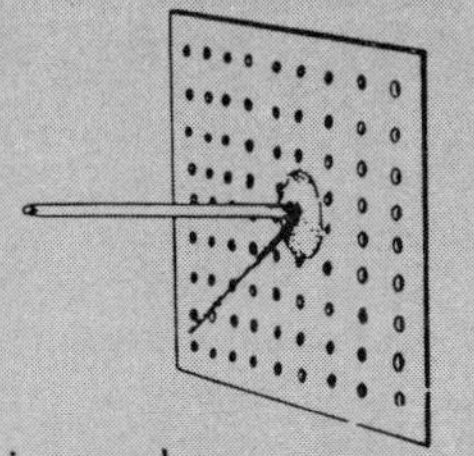

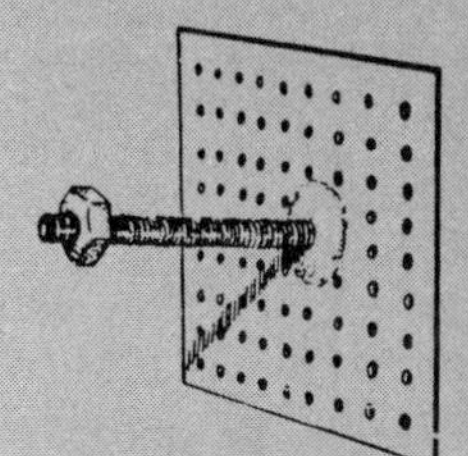

## STEPS FOR APPLICATION OF FURRING STRIPS

1 Dab of special adhesive is spread on perforated plate.
2 Plate is put on wall with slight twisting action. Let adhesive dry completely before proceeding.
3 Furring strips are impaled on the nail, and the nail is clinched.

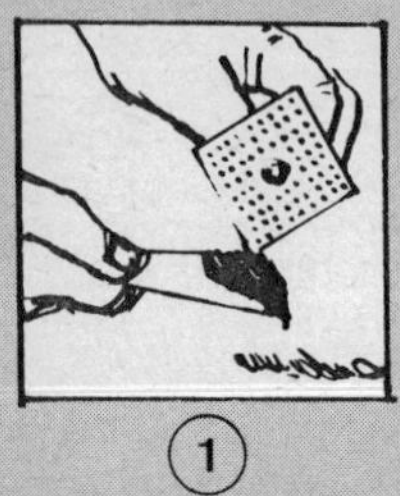

1

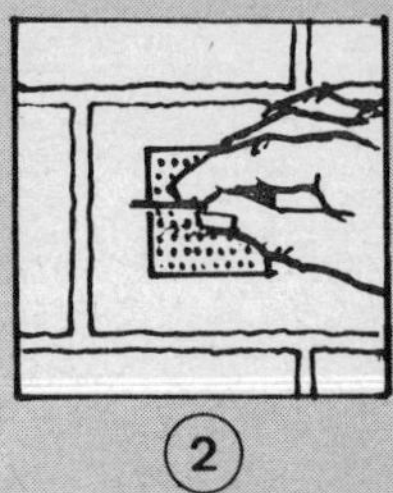

2

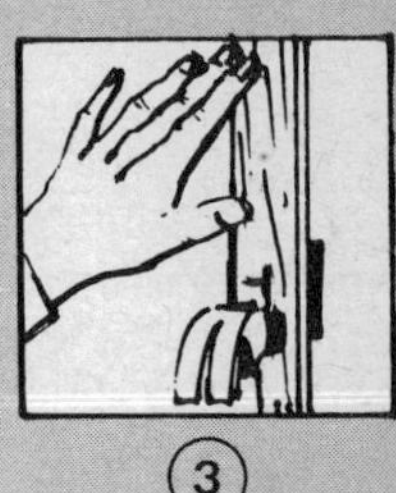

3

## PARTITION WALL THAT PROVIDES SOUNDPROOFING

1 2x6 or 2x8 sole plate
2 standard studs
3 insulation

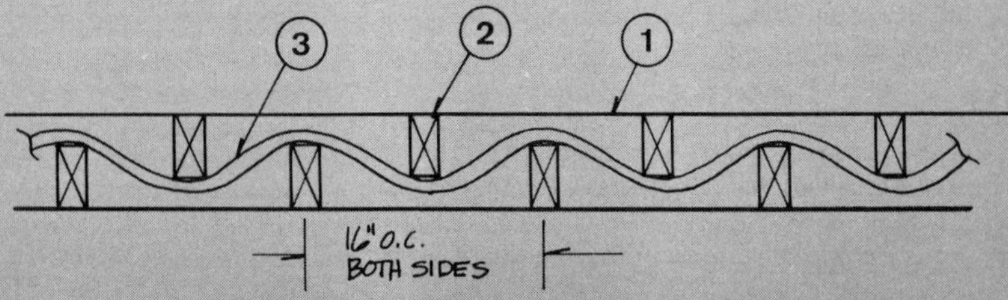

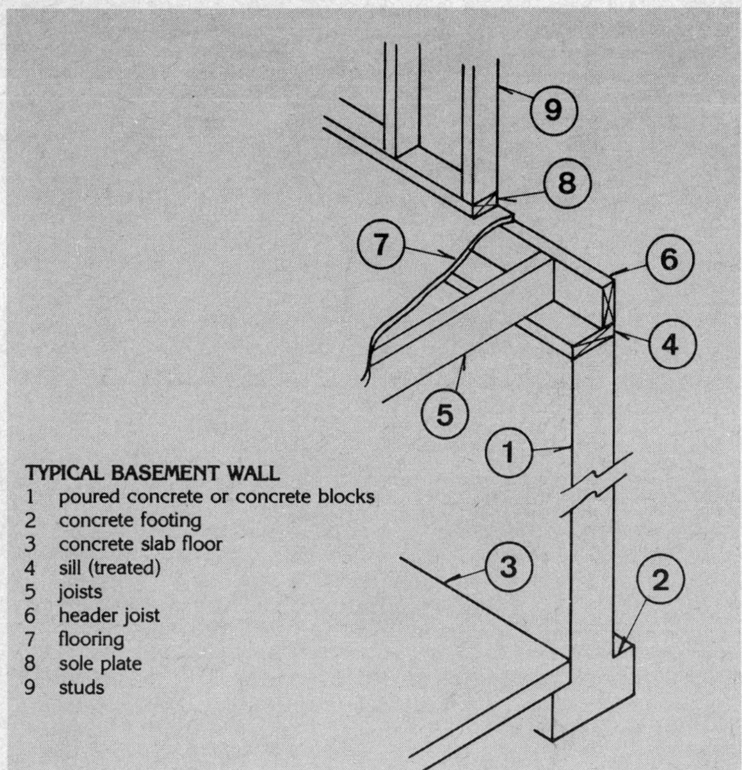


1x2 or 1x3 furring strips for wall paneling can be attached to masonry walls in various ways. A popular system uses anchor nails which stick with a special adhesive. Furring is hammered over the nail and the nail is clinched. Another way is attaching the furring directly to the masonry with case hardened nails. Rigid insulation can be applied with mastic directly to the walls — a good "extra." Cover furring with vapor barrier before applying paneling.

If you don't like the idea of walking on concrete you can create a wood floor by using one of the systems shown in the garage remodeling section.

Partitions are erected routinely — treated sole plate, studs, and top plate. Try to position partitions so they will hide any support columns that might be present. To cut down noise, say from a workshop or utility area to a living area, set up a soundproofing partition as shown in one of the drawings.

## ACOUSTICAL TILE CEILING

Acoustical tiles attach to 1x3 furring strips which are nailed at right angles to joists. On-center spacing of strips depends on the size of the tile.

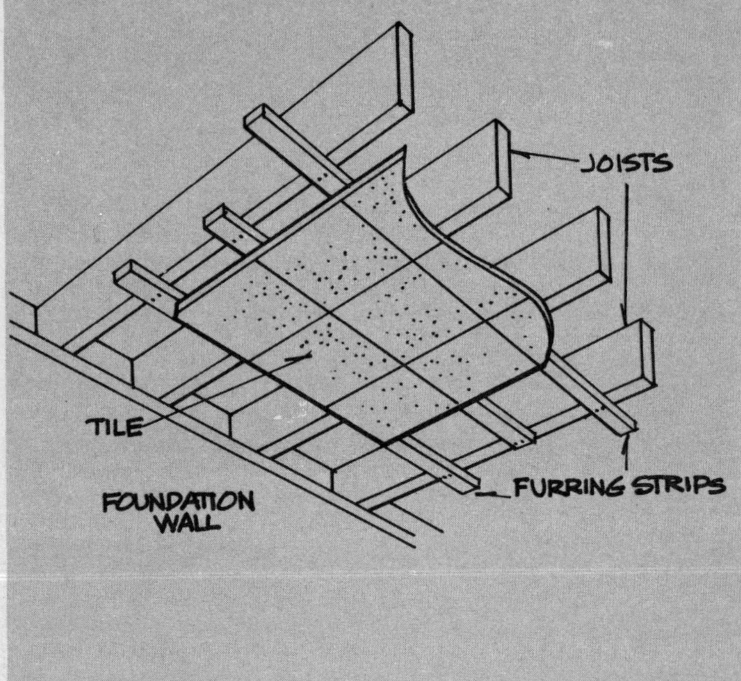


Ceilings can be done with gypsum wallboard if you wish to paint or with acoustical tiles if you want a more decorative look together with soundproofing. If joists are fairly uniform, tiles can be attached to furring strips that are nailed to the joists. If the levelness of the joists is a problem or if there are projections below the joist line — for example, pipes and heating ducts — a suspended ceiling might be the way to go.

The stairway to the basement will probably be a utility affair — just stringers and treads. This can be prettied up by adding risers and carpeting or hidden by a partition wall erected along the open end of the steps.

## SUSPENDED CEILING

The new ceiling is a gridwork of wood or metal strips that hang on wire from joists. The gridwork supports acoustical tiles.

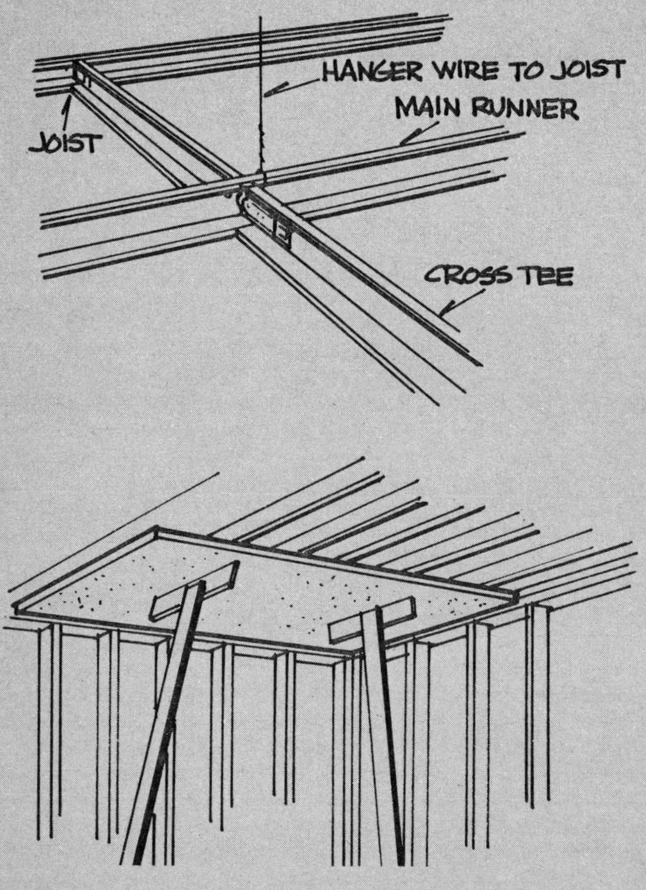


The chore of securing gypsum wallboard to ceiling joists will be much easier if you use T-braces to hold the panels while you nail.

# FOR MORE ROOM — THE ATTIC?

Many homes have attics that can be made livable in whole or in part. A basic criterion is whether there can be sufficient headroom — about 7½′ — over a reasonable area. But there are outs. For example, it is possible to construct a shed dormer which literally raises the roof and thus provides more floor space. Even when there is plenty of room, a shed dormer can be included as an outdoor area. What to do depends on space. With limited areas you may want a dormitory room for the children. With abundant space the options increase to things like a master bedroom with bath and a private deck, a child's room, or a private den. Stairways present space problems. If space is critical, consider a readymade folding stairway that can even be used in a hallway.

Subflooring can be applied directly to ceiling joists, but it should be carried to eaves' areas, since those places, after knee walls are erected and covered, can be used for storage. Ceiling joists can be added much as if they were collar beams. For a more dramatic look, run the ceiling right up to the ridge. The existing ridge probably won't be much to look at, so you'll want to bulk it (pieces on each side and a cap at the bottom) with handsome pieces of lumber. Another way is to run the ceiling up the rafters as high as possible and then go horizontal to hide the ridge.

Extra light and ventilation, if needed, can be supplied with simple dormers that will serve as windows. Do you want more light? Think of readymade skylights. Most are made to fit between standard rafter spacing so they can be installed without having to cut structural members. A good caulking job is critical; you don't want rain coming through the roof.

The overall appearance will depend on what you choose as wall and ceiling coverings. You can achieve a look anywhere from barn style to contemporary merely by choosing from the host of ready-to-apply, prefinished panelings that are available.

Don't neglect insulation. A remodeling of this nature puts you close to the sun and cold air.

A prefab freestanding fireplace or wood stove lends a cozy touch, but it must be located so the chimney can pass through the roof without affecting the ridge. If the unit requires a fireproof base, you can probably use slate, tile, or brick.

Access to the new attic room can be supplied simply by installing a readymade folding unit. It pulls down when needed. It can even be installed in a hallway.

A SHED DORMER CAN BE ORGANIZED THIS WAY TO PROVIDE A COVERED OUTDOOR AREA FOR THE NEW ROOM

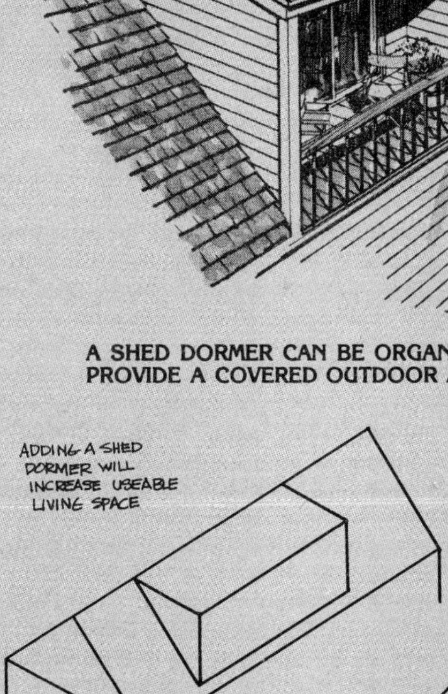

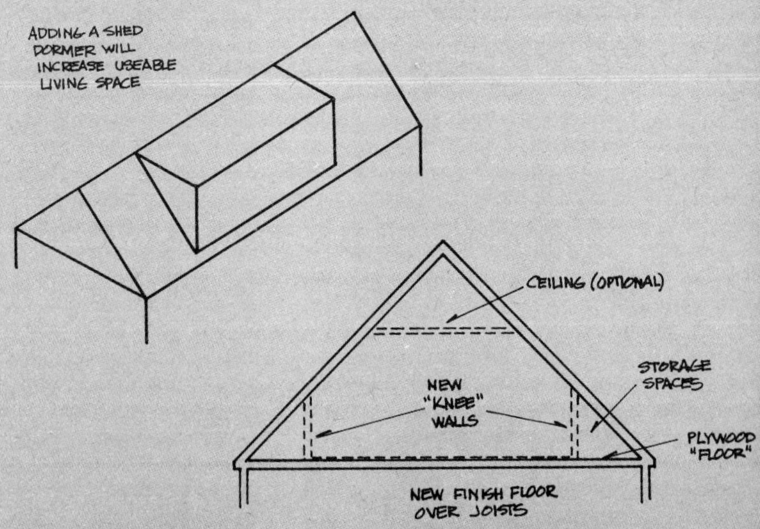

FRAMING DETAILS FOR A SHED DORMER

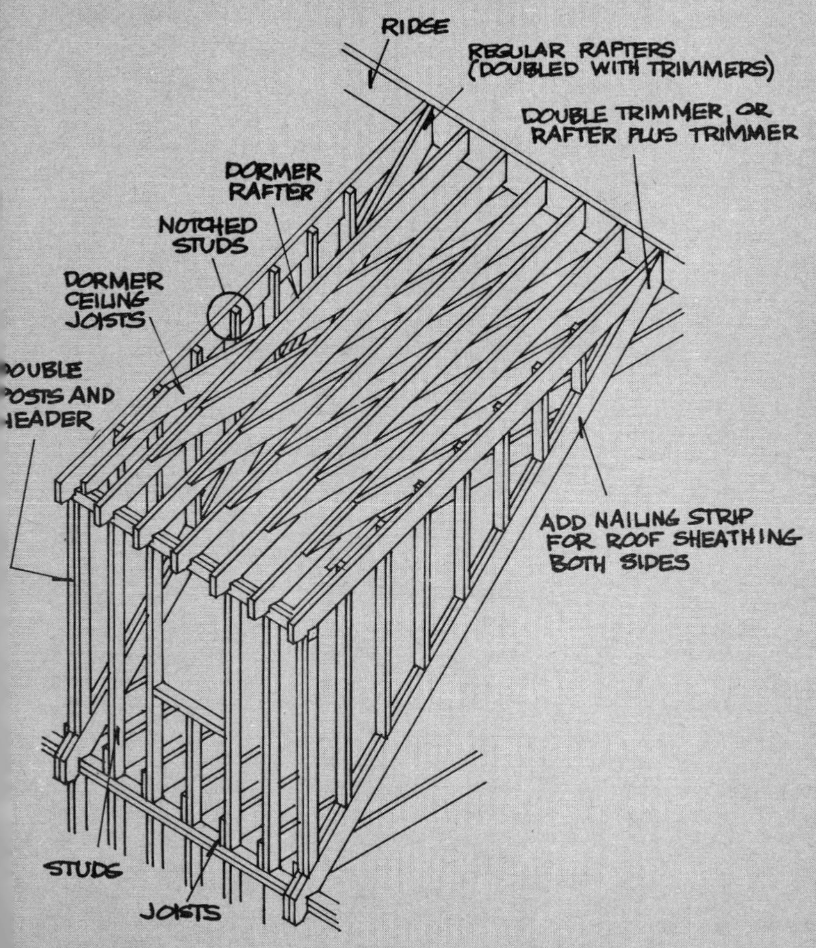

FRAMING DETAILS OF A DORMER THAT IS INCLUDED TO PROVIDE A WINDOW

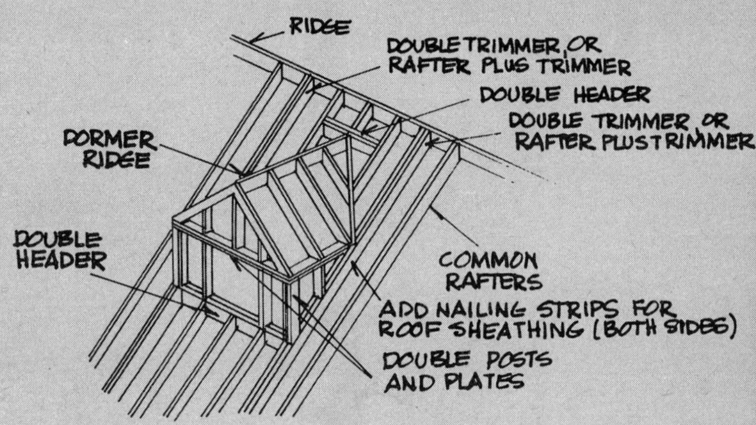


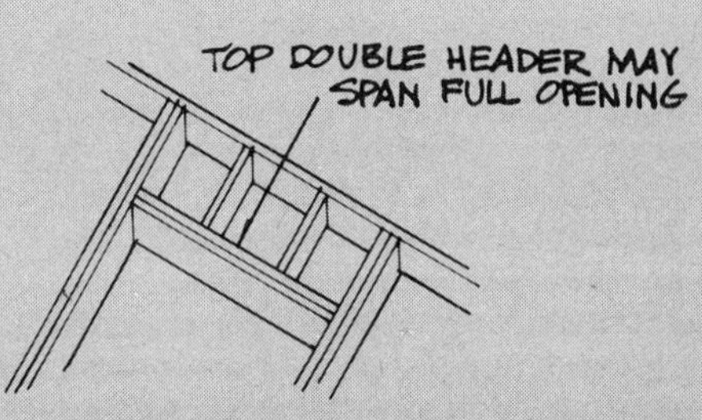

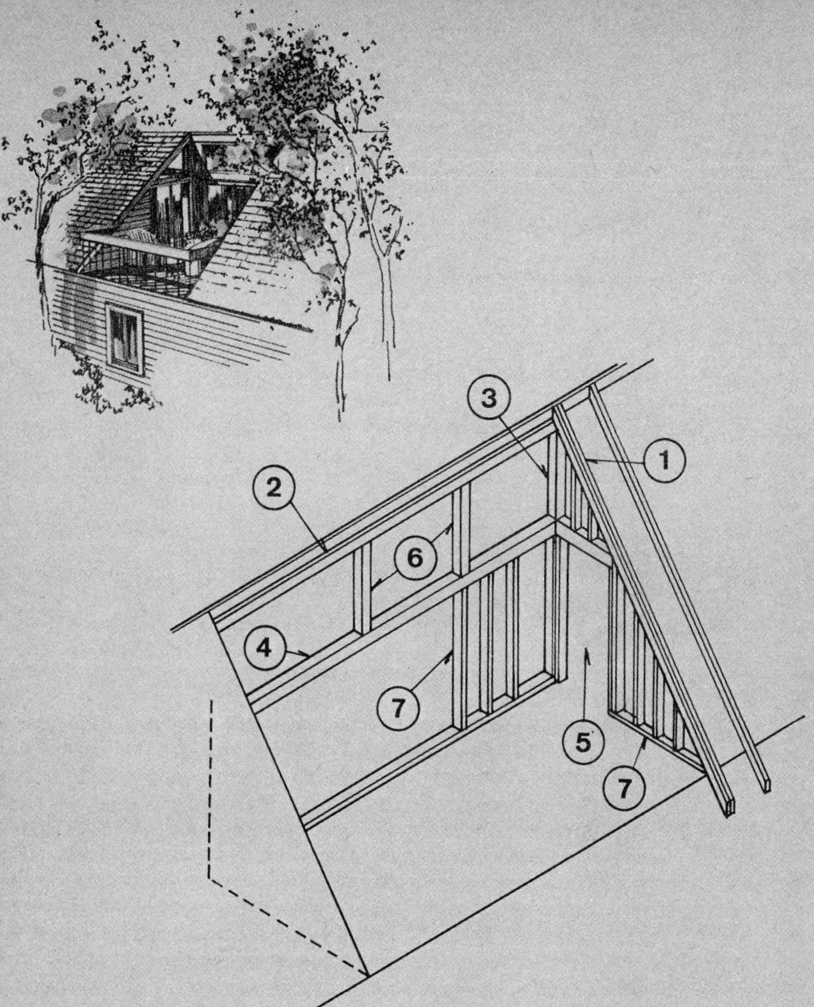


**AN OUTDOOR AREA AS PART OF THE NEW ATTIC ROOM**

1 The outline rafters are doubled (a trimmer is added).

2 Add a new 4x ridge (it can be left exposed).

3 4x4 posts

4 4x header

5 Opening for door — with standard header resting on trimmer studs.

6 4x4s — these, plus the new ridge and the header, provide framework for fixed glass.

7 standard wall framing

# INSECT-FREE OUTDOOR ROOM

You might call this project an organic room — insect control without the use of sprays. As designed, the room is over-built structurally, but the heavy beam work is attractive and reduces the number of elements to a minimum. If it seems too much, you can switch to a more conventional frame by keeping the heavy corner posts and upper perimeter pieces, but changing to 2x6 rafters and 2x4 studs.

The floor for the new room can be an existing patio or a specially poured slab. If a patio, sole plates can be set down on a bed of mastic and secured with case-hardened nails. If a new slab, prepare for the sole plate by setting anchor bolts in the concrete when it is poured. In either case, an alternate method is to secure posts with readymade post anchors. Like anchor bolts they can be set in fresh concrete. Attachment to an existing slab will call for drilling holes with a carbide-tipped masonry bit and using expansion sleeves and lag screws. The use of post anchors allows you to eliminate the sole plate if you wish.

Using framed screens secured with stops between posts is a practical way to go since it will not be difficult to replace or repair them should severe damage occur. Consider the use of readymade screen doors, available in 3′ widths and various styles.

The screens do not have to be the full height of the wall. Filling in part way up between posts with 2x4 sills and cripple studs will provide a frame for attaching plywood siding. If you go this way, plan the screen-opening so it will be suitable for using readymade window screens.

The roof cover can be a translucent material like fiberglass or it can be treated in a standard fashion — shingles over plywood sheathing. Exposed roof beams make a very attractive ceiling.

Another idea is to span the top beams with lattice work — spaced lath strips or 1x2s. These are very pretty when an attractive vine is trained to grow over them.

## INSECT-FREE OUTDOOR ROOM (cont'd)

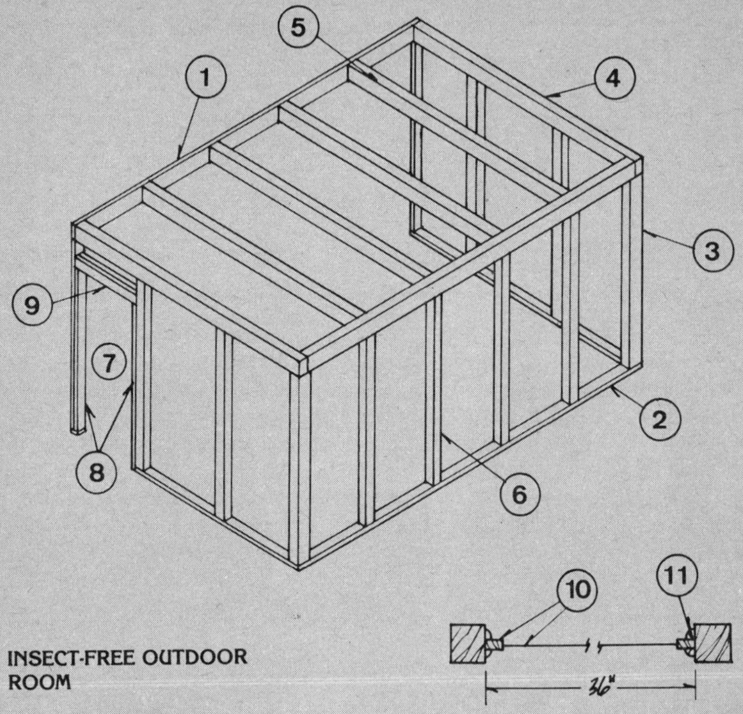


### INSECT-FREE OUTDOOR ROOM

1 2x6 ledger spiked or lag-screwed to house wall studs
2 2x4 sole plate (use pressure-treated lumber)
3 4x6 corner posts
4 top pieces all 4x6
5 beam hangers at each end
6 4x4 posts
7 door opening (optional)
8 trimmers
9 doubled 2x4 header

### SCREENS SHOULD BE PRE-FRAMED — INSTALLED AS UNITS

10 Framed screen (it's possible to use readymade screen doors).
11 Screens held in place with stops —make stops to suit or use ¼ round moulding.

Note . . . Top cover can be corrugated fiberglass panels or built-up roof (tar and gravel) or asphalt roofing over plywood roof sheathing.

# CONSTRUCTION TERMS YOU'LL NEED TO KNOW

The following diagrams illustrate the most common construction terms to know before entering into a building, remodeling, or decorating venture. (Of course, the more specific terms and problems are gone into at greater length in the individual projects.) A good working knowledge of building terms is invaluable for many reasons: to assess your home's present situation and what is feasible and desirable in the way of changes or additions; to read our project plans, and indeed, any kind of plan or blueprint; to be familiar with the terminology of contractors or other experts; to know the major construction components that relate to building materials.

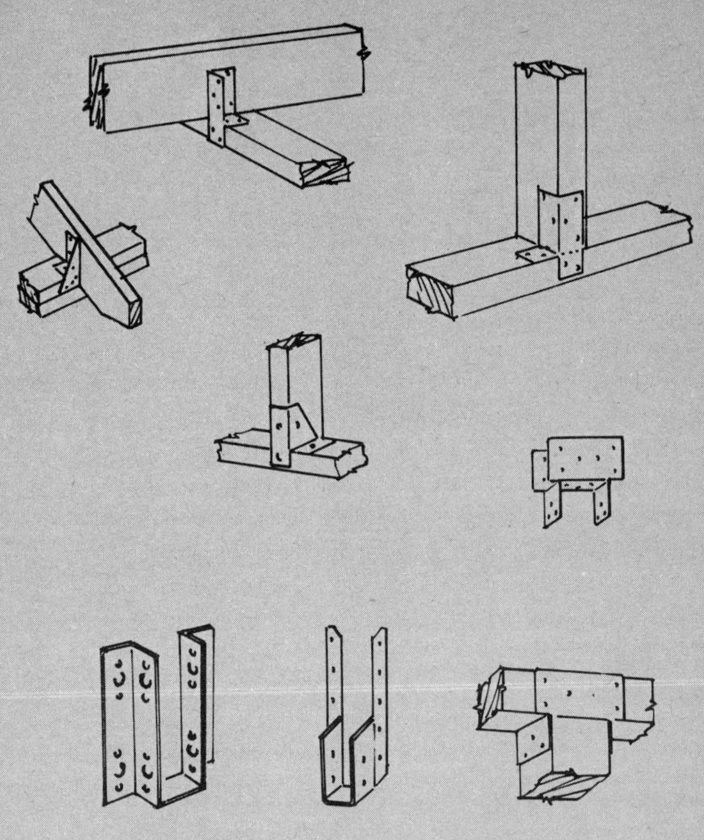

## FRAMING ANCHORS AND HANGERS

Readymade pieces of hardware make house-framing chores easier. Units usually identified by application. For example, "joist anchor," "rafter anchor," "post base."

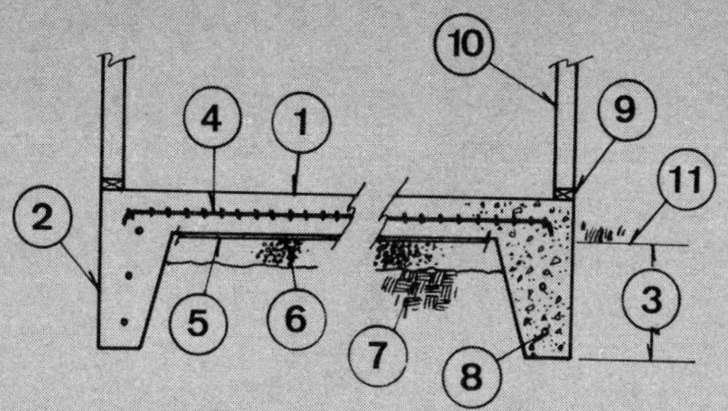


**A CONCRETE SLAB TO BUILD ON**

1 slab thickness 4″ to 6″
2 integral footings
3 footings to extend below the frost line
4 reinforcement (welded wire fabric)
5 vapor barrier (4 or 6 mil plastic sheeting)
6 compacted gravel sub base
7 firm subgrade
8 reinforcement bars
9 sole plate — treated lumber (tied to slab with anchor bolts)
10 wall studs
11 grade

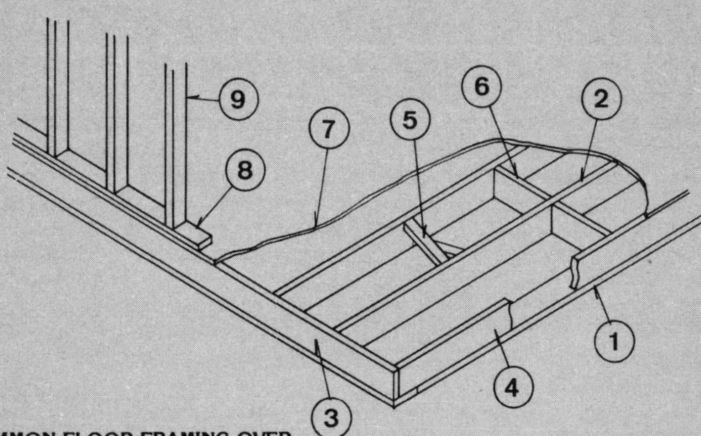


**COMMON FLOOR FRAMING OVER A CRAWL SPACE OR BASEMENT**

1 2x6 sill (treated)
2 2x joists (width depends on span — intermediate post/beam supports often required on long spans)
3 2x header joist
4 2x stringer joist
5 bridging (not always used, especially if subfloor will be heavy plywood)
6 alternate method of doing bridging
7 subfloor
8 sole plate
9 studs

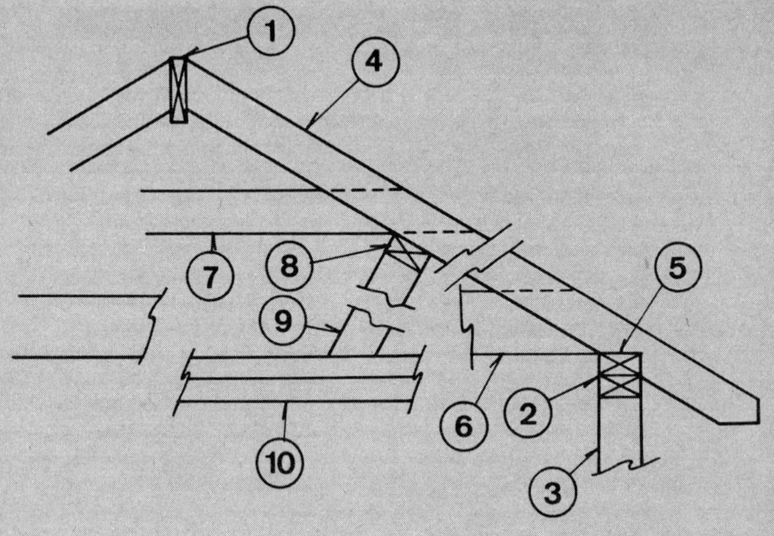


## ROOF FRAMING

1 ridge
2 top (rafter) plate
3 studs
4 rafters
5 cut in rafter over plate is called "bird's mouth"
6 2x6 or wider ceiling joists
7 1x6 collar beam
8 2x4 purlin
9 2x4 brace
10 bearing partition (preferably)

Note . . . Purlins used mostly when rafters are very long and will be more stable with mid-point support.

## ROOF RAFTERS

1 top (rafter) plate
2 ridge
3 common rafters
4 hip rafters
5 valley rafters
6 jack rafters
7 cripples
8 overhang (eaves)

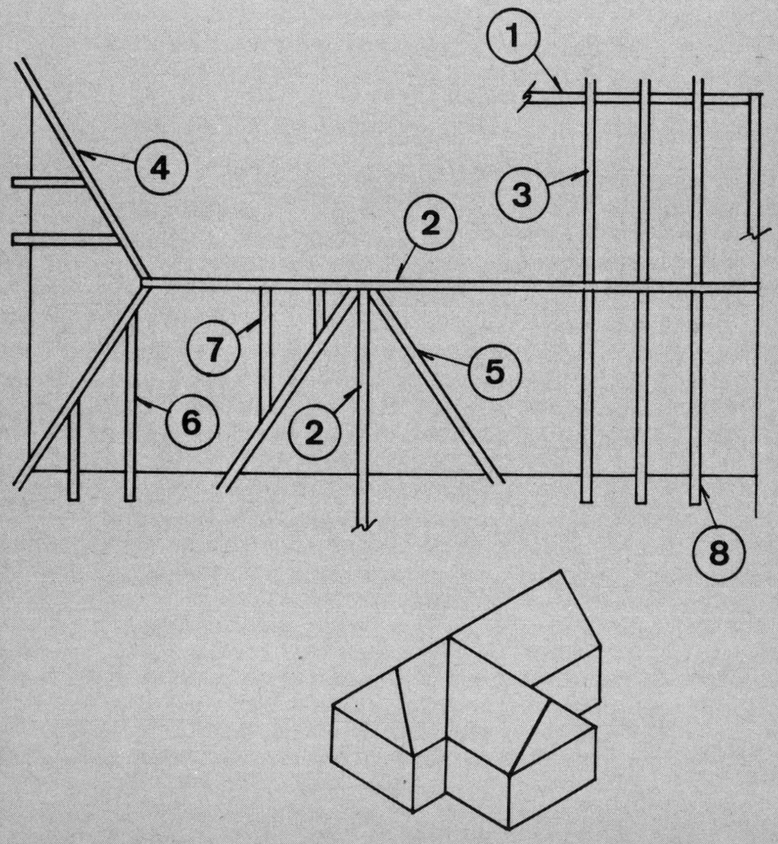

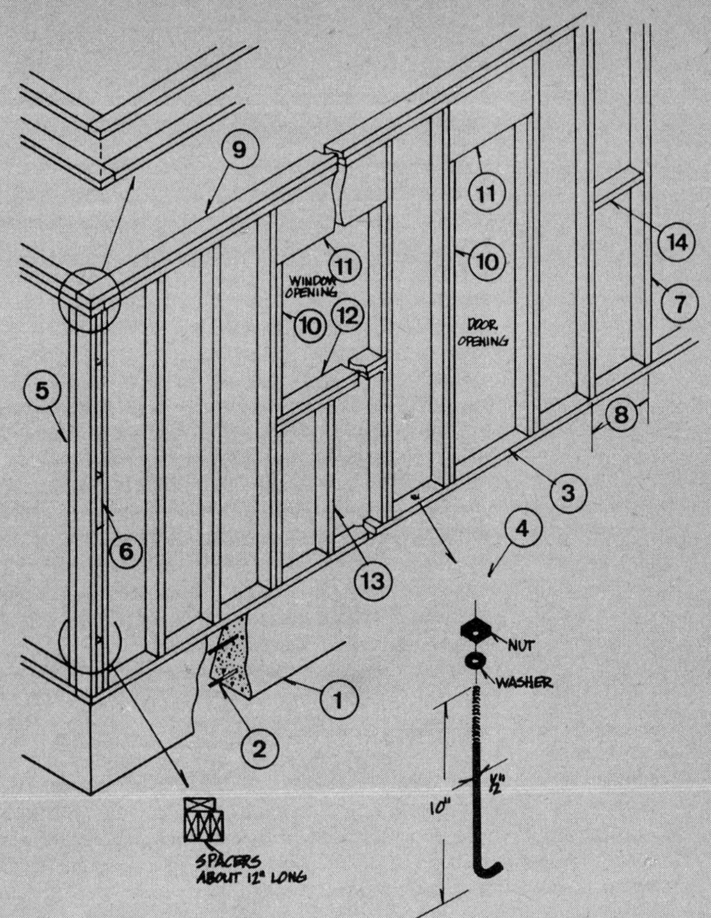


## COMMON WALL FRAMING

(Sole plate attachment is typical for a concrete slab.)

1 foundation
2 reinforcement rods
3 2x4 sole or base plate (treated)
4 anchor bolts
5 corner post assembly (all 2x4s)
6 3 spacers
7 2x4 studs
8 stud spacing — 16″ on centers typical
9 doubled 2x4 top or rafter plate
10 2x4 trimmers
11 4x12 headers
12 doubled 2x4 rough sill
13 2x4 cripples
14 fire stops — optional (check local codes)

# 2/ EASY-TO-BUILD PROJECTS

Extra! Extra! Read all about our broad range of projects — 25 in all — that will add a touch of personality to your home, indoors and out. We've included technical drawings and instructions to help you build any (or all) of these projects right from the book. There are also helpful materials lists to simplify shopping at your Georgia-Pacific Registered Dealer. The projects offer you the chance to beautify your home and at the same time to add to it practical and serviceable elements. We know that no matter what you build, you'll experience the joys of making your home a better place to live.

# COFFEE TABLE plus SEATS

The table and seats are a neat and practical ensemble, but of course you can choose to make either. Use-options can affect materials. For a formal result, work with a fancy hardwood plywood like walnut or mahogany or birch. If, for example, the project will be used in a child's room where it might be abused, a paintable plywood like pine or top-grade fir and a table surface veneered with a plastic laminate make sense.

## THE TABLE

Start by cutting the top to exact size and then covering its edges with matching wood strips that are rabbeted as shown in the detail drawing. It's wise to cut these strips longer than necessary; trim them to exact size as they are applied. Work with glue and a few 6d casing nails.

Next — cut the parts (#3 and 4) for the top crosspiece and accurately mark its location on the underside of the table top. Make the attachment with glue and a few 6d casing nails. The glue does the job; nails are used merely to keep the pieces positioned.

Cut the parts for the pedestals to the sizes listed in the bill of materials and put them together as separate assemblies. Careful work is required here since the miter cuts must be exact. Testing cuts on scrap stock before cutting good material makes sense. Assemble the parts with glue and 4d finishing nails, setting the nails only as deep as necessary so they can be hidden with wood dough. The pedestals are then attached to the top crosspiece with glue and 6d finishing nails.

The final step is to make the bottom crosspiece. Attach it with glue and 6d finishing nails.

## THE SEATS

These are simple boxes, but call for careful work because of the miter joints. Cut all sides and the corner blocks to size. Begin assembly by using glue and 4d casing nails to attach the corner blocks to opposite sides of the seat. Then add the remaining two sides, using glue and 6d finishing nails for the attachment.

Cut the top pieces to size and add them to the assembly. These rest on and are nailed into the top ends of the corner blocks. Two 6d finishing nails through each side should be added.

Top pads are foam rubber covered with a material of your choice. Attach the foam rubber with rubber cement; be careful when folding the cover material at corners.

Another way to supply a pad — make or buy cushions that are 2″ thick and 16″ square. Attach them with tufting buttons — large decorative buttons that are secured with strong twine that is needled through the cushion. In this case, small holes for the twine must be drilled through the top of the seat. An advantage of the tufted cushions is that they are easily replaced.

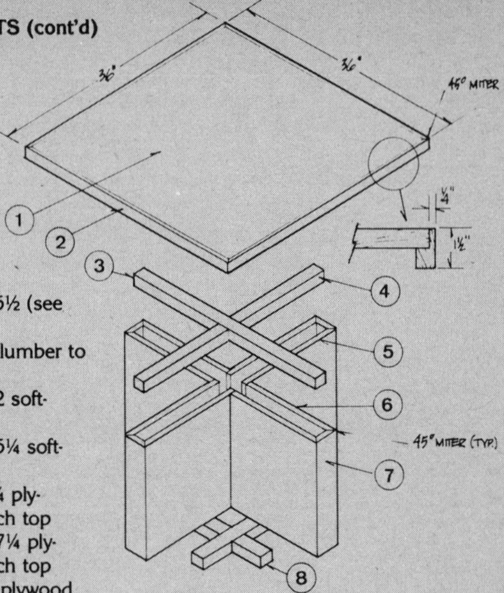

## COFFEE TABLE PLUS SEATS (cont'd)

### COFFEE TABLE

**Materials List**

(Actual dimensions. See chart page 187.)

| | | |
|---|---|---|
| 1 | 1 pc. | ¾ x 35½ x 35½ (see text) |
| 2 | 4 pcs. | ¾ x 1½ x 36 lumber to match top |
| 3 | 1 pc. | 1½ x 1½ x 32 softwood lumber |
| 4 | 2 pcs. | 1½ x 1½ x 15¼ softwood lumber |
| 5 | 4 pcs. | ¾ x 16 x 17¼ plywood to match top |
| 6 | 4 pcs. | ¾ x 15¼ x 17¼ plywood to match top |
| 7 | 4 pcs. | ¾ x 3 x 17¼ plywood to match top |
| 8 | to brace bottom of pedestals — make from strips of 1½" stock or cut as one unit from a piece of 2 x 12 x 12 softwood lumber | |

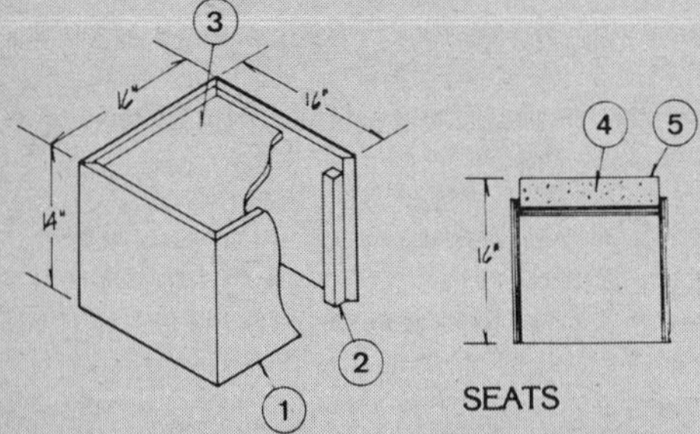


### SEATS

| | | |
|---|---|---|
| 1 | 16 pcs. | ¾ x 14 x 16 plywood to match table |
| 2 | 16 pcs. | 1 x 1 x 13¼ softwood lumber |
| 3 | 4 pcs. | ¾ x 14½ x 14½ plywood |
| 4 | 4 pcs. | 2 x 16 x 16 (foam rubber) |
| 5 | 4 pcs. | about 24" square (cover material) |

# WALL-HUNG UTILITY DESK

Build this project in the shop as a complete unit, then hang it anywhere — in the kitchen for planning menus, in a child's room as a convenient, minimum-space desk, wherever. To attach to a wall, drive 4 #10 x 1¾″ long flat head screws through the back of the project into wall studs. Take care that the writing surface will not be more than 28″ or 29″ above the floor. It can be lower for a child — and it can be raised as the child grows.

Materials can be paintable lumber or a plywood that harmonizes with existing wall paneling or cabinetry. If plywood, use a matching veneer wood-tape to cover all visible edges.

Start work by cutting sides and ends of the case to length, then carefully form the corner miters. Rabbet the back edge of each case piece to receive the recessed back. Assemble case pieces with white glue and 4d finishing nails; add the back, using glue and 2d box nails.

Cut horizontal and vertical shelf pieces to size and add to the case by using glue and 6d finishing nails. Final step is to cut the door/writing surface to size and to install it with the flap hinges and the lid supports that are shown in detail in the drawing. The flap hinges may be difficult to find, but they can be ordered for you. If there is a problem, substitute a length of continuous hinge, but reduce the height of the door and the width of the bottom case-piece by ¾″.

Use one or two magnetic catches to secure the door in raised position.

Options — cover the writing surface with a solid color plastic laminate (using contact cement); face the back of the writing area and the larger area above it with ½″-thick cork. The soft surface can be used like a bulletin board.

## WALL-HUNG UTILITY DESK (cont'd)

## WALL-HUNG UTILITY DESK

### Materials List

(Actual dimensions. See chart page 187.)

| | | |
|---|---|---|
| 1 | 2 pcs. | ¾ x 8 x 48 plywood or lumber |
| 2 | 2 pcs. | ¾ x 8 x 24 plywood or lumber |
| 3 | 1 pc. | ¼ x 23¼ x 47¼ plywood |
| 4 | 2 pcs. | ¾ x 7¾ x 22½ plywood or lumber |
| 5 | 1 pc. | ¾ x 16 x 7¾ plywood or lumber |
| 6 | 1 pc. | ¾ x 6 x 7¾ plywood or lumber |
| 7 | 1 pc. | ¾ x 16 x 22½ plywood |
| | 2 | flap hinges |
| | 2 | lid supports |

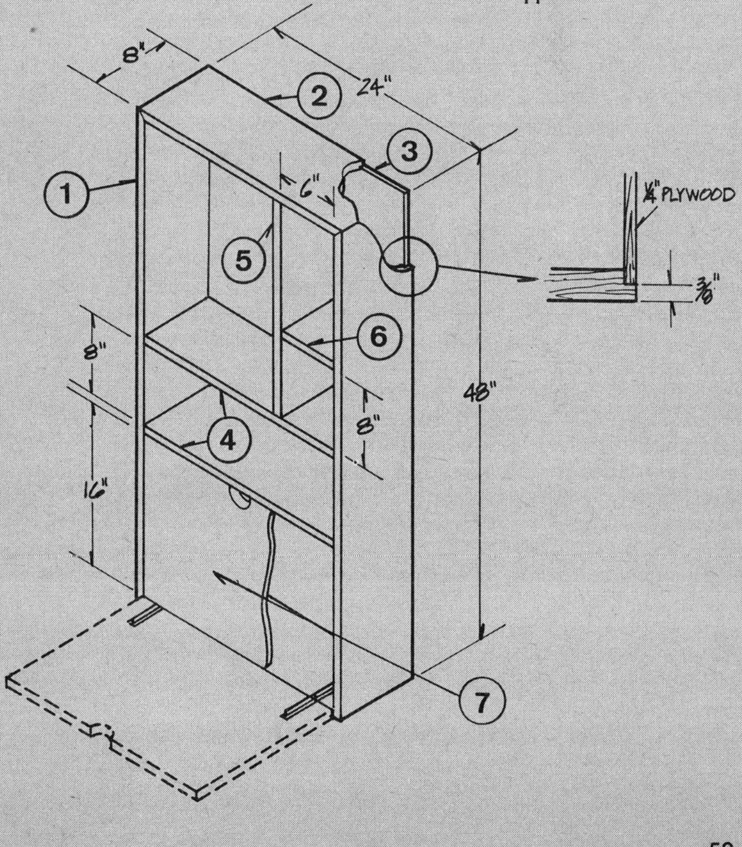

# PARTITION SCREEN

A partition screen can make sense in many areas — a block between a toilet and sink area, a "wall" to create a nook for a dressing table or desk, a projection into a room as a backing for a chair or even a bed. It can be designed as a decor accent or finished to blend with existing walls. It's a quick and simple construction project that requires only 2x4 framing (or 2x2 framing if you wish to save space) and your choice of prefinished wall paneling, gypsum board (to paint or wallpaper), or lumber.

Secure the sole plate by nailing into the floor, the top plate by nailing into joists. Use a plumb bob to be sure the plates are correctly aligned. Add the studs; three full-length ones for a solid wall — additional framing (as shown in the drawings) if you wish to have a see-through section or a mirror.

The drawings also list the kind of mouldings you can use for that finished, professional look. If you are using prefinished wall paneling, you can either choose from harmonizing prefinished mouldings, or mouldings to stain or paint. If you are using gypsum wallboard or lumber, there are similar unfinished mouldings available.

## PARTITION SCREEN

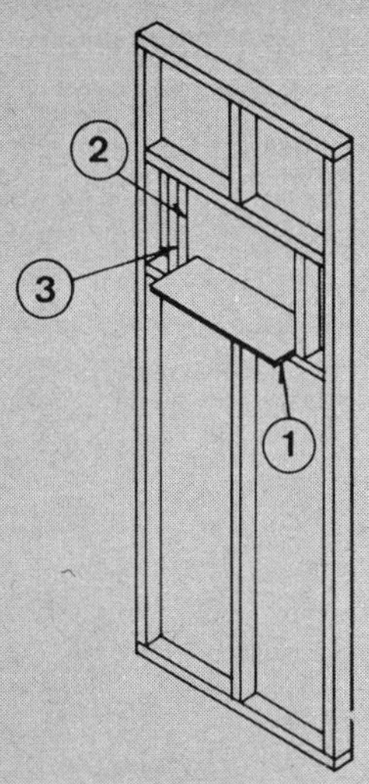


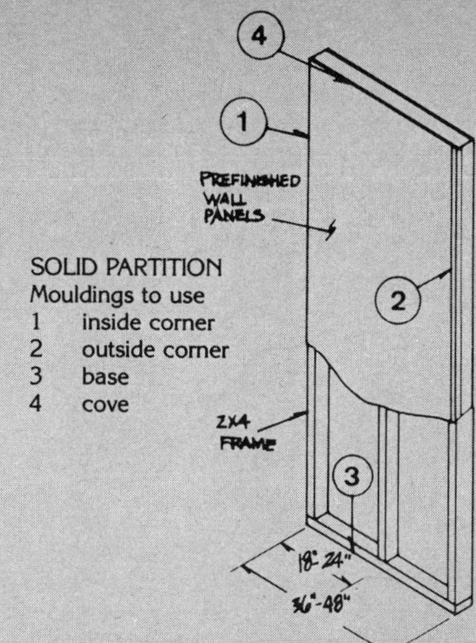


A SOLID PARTITION
Mouldings to use
1 inside corner
2 outside corner
3 base
4 cove

B FRAMED FOR SEE-THRU AREA WITH SHELF FOR POTTED PLANT OR BRIC-A-BRAC
1 ¾″ lumber shelf
2 paneling
3 outside corner moulding

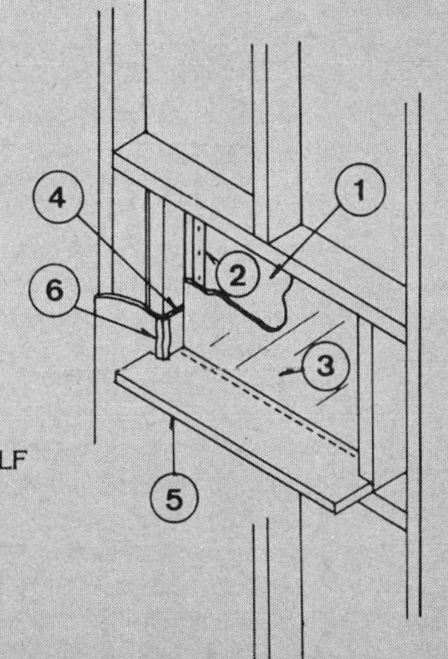


C FRAMING FOR A MIRROR WITH SHELF
1 back of paneling
2 ¾″ lumber as stops
3 mirror
4 paneling
5 ¾″ lumber shelf
6 outside corner moulding

# GARDEN BENCH

This is a simple design, but effective and sturdy. It can be installed in a permanent location or made portable; the only difference will be in the length of the posts required for the legs. In either case, legs and rails are put together as separate assemblies. If clamps are available, use them to hold rails to legs as you drill the holes for the carriage bolts. Then separate the parts, clean away wood chips, and reassemble after coating mating surfaces with waterproof glue. Take up on the carriage-bolt nuts only as much as is needed to bring parts firmly together.

Cut all parts for the seat-slab to size and assemble as follows. Glue and nail a spacer to one outside bench board. Add the second bench board and then the second spacer and so on. Use waterproof glue and galvanized nails at each connection. Use 4d nails to attach spacers; use 8d nails through bench boards. Attach the end boards with glue and two 8d nails at each bearing.

Mark the location of the leg assemblies on the slab and then coat the top surfaces of rails and legs with glue. Put the slab in place and then drive the four 6d nails, locating them so they will penetrate a rail, not the top of the leg. Pilot holes for the nails are a must. Driving them without the precaution will split the wood.

The drawing detail shows how legs can be installed in soil. It's a good idea, regardless of what type of wood you chose to work with, to treat the buried portion with a preservative — or you can work with a wood that has been pressure-treated to resist insects and decay.

Various grades of redwood are popular for outside projects, but there are options. Pine, fir, and cedar are attractive and may be more plentiful in various areas of the country.

GARDEN BENCH

**Materials List**

(Actual dimensions. See chart page 187.)

| | | |
|---|---|---|
| bench boards | 10 | 1½ x 3½ x 60 lumber |
| end boards | 2 | ¾ x 3½ x 19½ lumber |
| spacers | 2 | ½ x 3½ x 5 lumber |
| | 2 | ½ x 3½ x 8 lumber |
| | 2 | ½ x 3½ x 11 lumber |
| | 2 | ½ x 3½ x 14 lumber |
| | 1 | ½ x 3½ x 17 lumber |
| legs | 4 | 3½ x 3½ x 14½ lumber |
| rails | 4 | 1½ x 3½ x 19½ lumber |

Note . . . For fixed installation increase leg-lengths by amount that will be buried. Use treated lumber for this application.

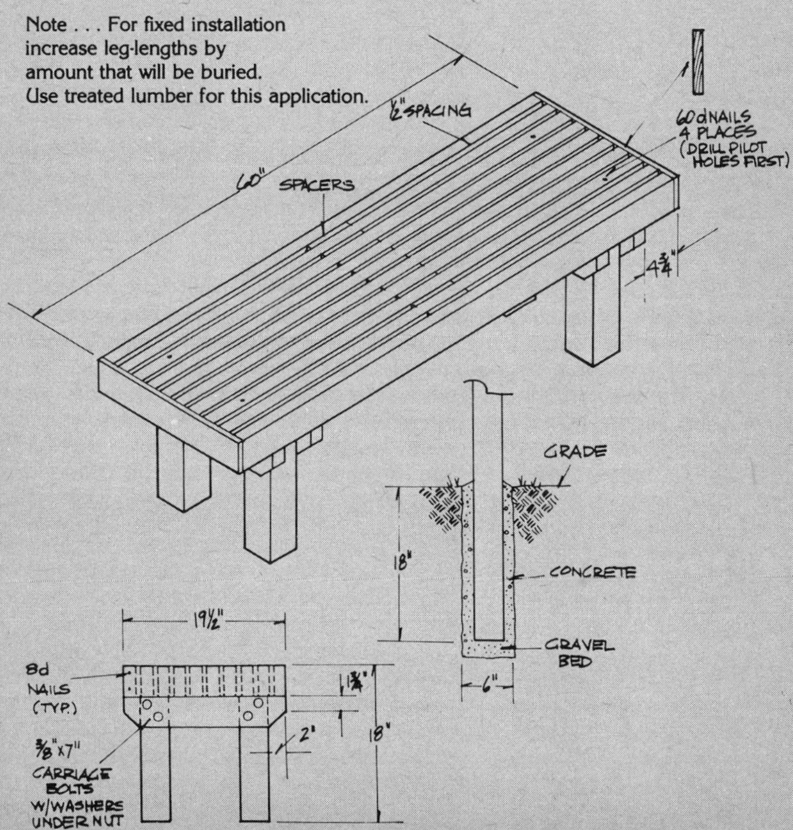

# PLANTER TREES

A planter tree is a unique way to display special plants. Place it permanently in the ground or give it a base that permits its use anywhere. Design it with supports so pots can hang from a chain, or with shelves so pots just sit.

For in-ground placement you can work with a pressure-treated post or choose any species — pine or fir, redwood or cedar. Treating soil-contact areas with a preservative is a wise precaution even though the latter two have a natural resistance against decay and insect damage.

Spacing between shelves or supports depends on the size of the pots and the type of plants you wish to display. A permanent installation for pots that will hang from a chain can be taller than the six feet suggested. Seven or even eight feet above grade is not out of line and can be very dramatic.

Be sure to use a waterproof glue in all joints in addition to the nails called for. Holes for supports should be sized to provide a tight fit for the material that is used. If a dowel is used, it should be sealed or stained or painted to match the post. Aluminum holds up okay outdoors, but a pipe or a steel rod should be treated with a clear, protective spray or, maybe, painted wrought-iron black. The latter thought also applies to the chain used to hang pots unless you use a type that has a galvanized coating.

Even if you plan a natural look, all wood parts should be treated with an exterior type sealer.

## PLANTER TREES

A permanent in-ground placement

B base for indoor/outdoor movable unit

C Supports for pots suspended with chain; can be heavy dowel, aluminum tubing, pipe, steel rods.

D Pots can sit on shelves if the unit is made this way.

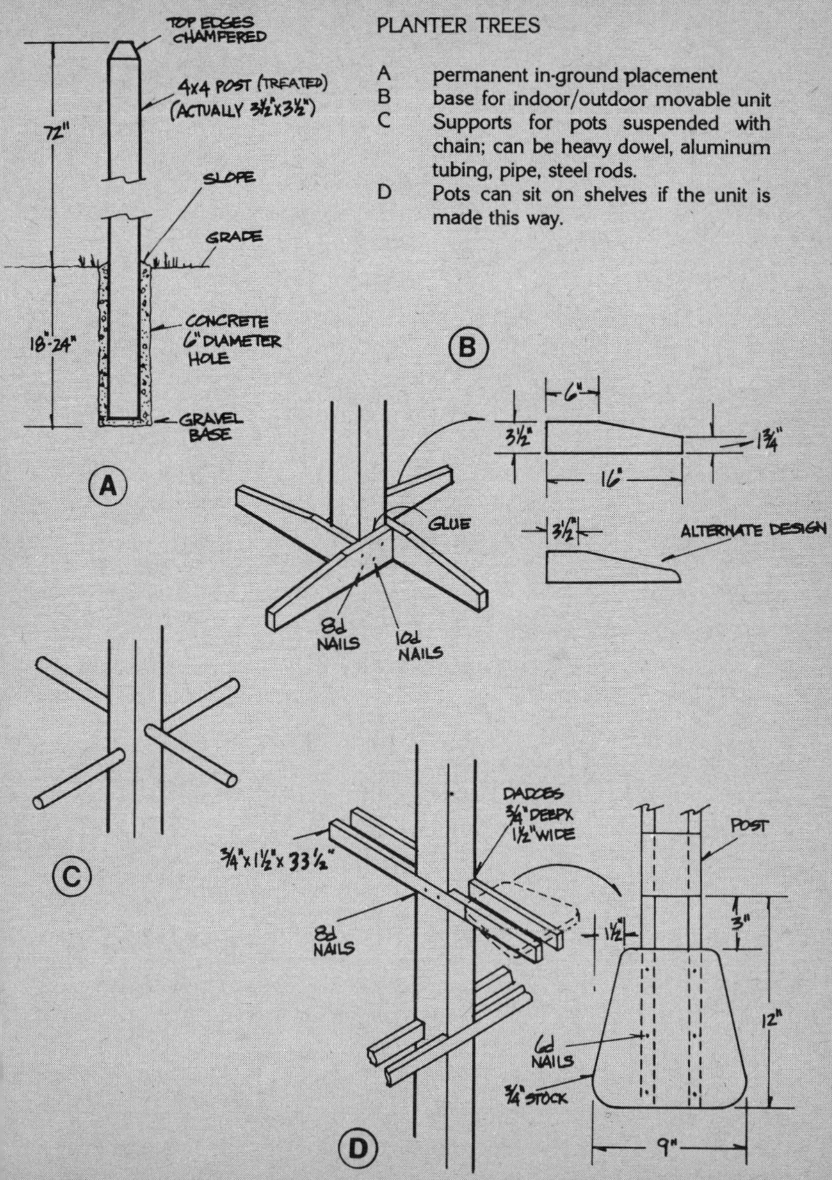

# HEY KIDS — YOUR OWN PLAYGROUND! (Any Parent Can Build It)

Here's a special environment for youngsters, whether they like to climb, exercise, have lunch in a private treehouse, or play in sand; and it's steps away from your own back door.

First step — lay out the area for locations of the main 10′ long posts, then dig 6″ diameter holes, 24″ deep. Don't form the holes with a shovel; an auger or a clamshell digger you can rent is better since either will disturb less soil, and there will be less concrete to pour. Place a 3″ layer of gravel in the hole, set the posts, and fill around them with concrete. Use a level on two adjacent sides of each post to be sure they are plumb; add temporary braces to hold them until the concrete sets — about 24 hours. The three remaining posts (parts 7 and 9) can be set at this time, or you can wait so they can be more easily established with other components. No matter when you do it, they are set in the ground like the main posts.

The next step is to add the joists that will support the deck. Start with the main ones (#2), attaching them with 16d nails. Add numbers 3 and 4, also with 16d nails. The deck boards can be square-edge pieces or tongue-and-groove material. Either way, each board is attached with three 16d nails at each bearing point. Final steps for the main part of the project are adding the sand-box boards and the top rail. Here too, use 16d nails at mating points.

The stringers for the ladder (#10) should be a strong material — something like kiln-dried, straight-grain fir; the rungs can be a closet pole (actually a large diameter dowel), aluminum tubing or ordinary plumbing pipe. If dowel, secure with glue and a 10d nail as shown in the detail drawing. If tubing or pipe, drill a hole first, then use a sheet metal screw that is long enough to penetrate one wall of the material. The same thinking applies to the rungs (#8) of the vertical ladder.

The top end of the ladder is secured with ½" x 6" carriage bolts. This permits it to swivel so it can be raised and be supported by the two outboard posts (#9) for use as a horizontal swing ladder. To establish this secondary position, have someone hold the ladder in a horizontal posture while you drill for the carriage bolts. You can provide more interest if you drill additional holes for the carriage bolts so the ladder can be secured at various angles. For example, you can secure it at 15 degrees and at 45 degrees.

MATERIALS

Posts should be pressure-treated to protect against decay and insect damage. The boards that form the sand box should also be pressure-treated lumber. Deck boards, joists, top rails can be pine, redwood, fir — there are many options. It is important that all materials be S4S — sanded four sides — no splinters allowed!

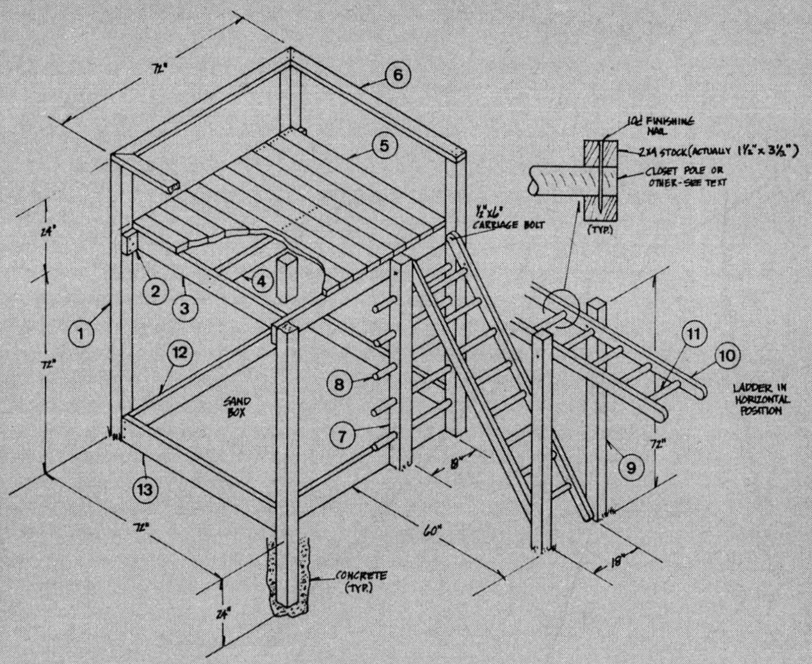


## PLAYGROUND

### Materials List

(Actual dimensions. See chart page 187.)

| | | |
|---|---|---|
| 1 | 4 pcs. | 3½ x 3½ x 120 lumber |
| 2 | 2 pcs. | 1½ x 5½ x 72 lumber |
| 3 | 2 pcs. | 1½ x 5½ x 62 lumber |
| 4 | 1 pc. | 1½ x 5½ x 62 lumber |
| 5 | 12 pcs. | 1½ x 5½ x 65 lumber |
| 6 | 3 pcs. | 1½ x 3½ x 72 lumber |
| 7 | 1 pc. | 3½ x 3½ x 94½ lumber |
| 8 | 5 pcs. | rungs = 31″ long (dowel) |
| 9 | 2 pcs. | 3½ x 3½ x 96 lumber |
| 10 | 2 pcs. | 1½ x 3½ x 120 straight-grain fir Check and cut to exact length on assembly. |
| 11 | 8 pcs. | rungs = 18″ long (dowel) |
| 12 | 2 pcs. | 1½ x 7¼ x 69 lumber (treated) |
| 13 | 2 pcs. | 1½ x 7¼ x 65 lumber (treated) |
| | 4 | ½″ x 6″ carriage bolts w/washers and nuts |

# BATHROOM BENCH

The project provides a place for a magazine or book, a dish of special soap, a bottle of lotion — whatever you might want near you while enjoying a hot tub. It's also convenient for sitting while drying toes.

Lumber is called for — for example, clear pine if you end up by painting, or a hardwood like mahogany or walnut or birch if you plan a natural finish.

Start the project by forming the two top end-pieces and attaching them to the top slab with waterproof glue and 6d finishing nails. Next, make the base, shaping the ends as shown in the detail drawing.

Each pedestal consists of two parts which are joined in a 45 degree miter that is reinforced with glue and 3d finishing nails.

Put together the top, base and pedestals by using glue and 6d finishing nails. Be sure to go over all surfaces and edges with fine sandpaper before applying a finish. The project should not appear to have sharp corners. Round off all corners, slightly at least, by working with the sandpaper.

BATHROOM BENCH

**Materials List**

(Actual dimensions. See chart page 187.)

| | | |
|---|---|---|
| 1 | 1 pc. | ¾ x 10 x 14½ lumber |
| 2 | 2 pcs. | ¾ x 2 x 10 lumber |
| 3 | 1 pc. | ¾ x 10 x 16 lumber |
| 4 | 4 pcs. | ¾ x 5 x 12½ lumber |

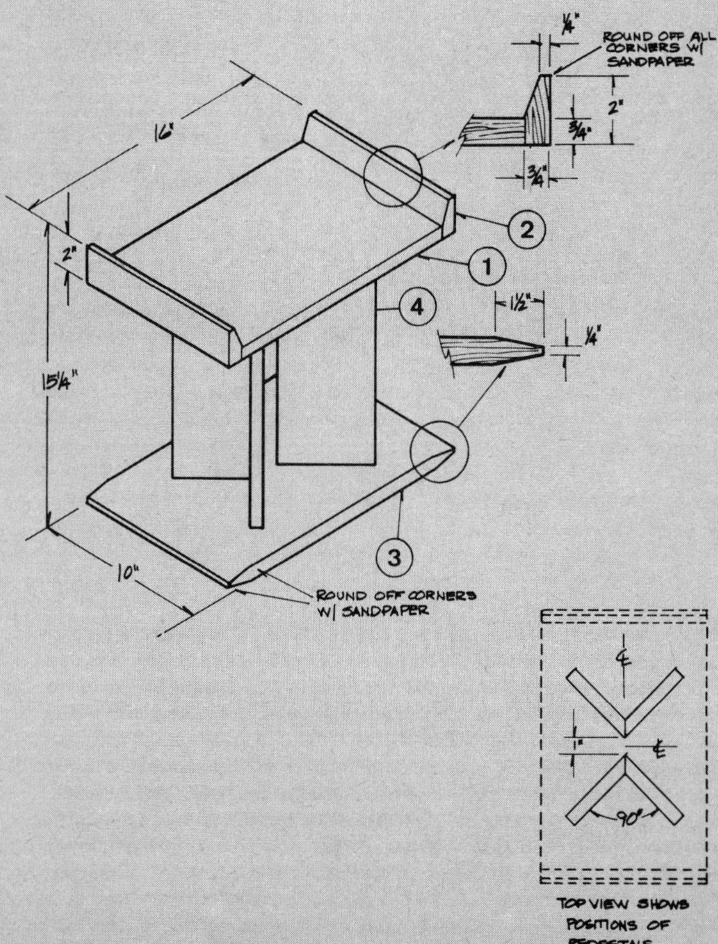

# FIRESIDE BENCH

It's handy because it provides for extra seating as well as storage for logs and kindling and magazines. The design has a 1″ high perimeter "wall" which forms a pocket for a pad. If you use a 2″ thick pad, the total height of the project will be 18″ — comfortable for sitting.

All material is ¾″ plywood except for the front frame pieces which are cut from lumber. All joints are butted and reinforced with glue and 8d finishing nails through plywood parts, 6d finishing nails through the lumber pieces.

Cut all plywood parts to size and then follow this order of assembly: back to sides, then the bottom, followed by the top and the two dividers.

It's a good idea when doing the frame to cut parts longer than necessary. Trim them to exact length as you add them to the project.

Plywood edges will be exposed on the top edges of the back and the sides. You can finish those edges with strips of veneer banding.

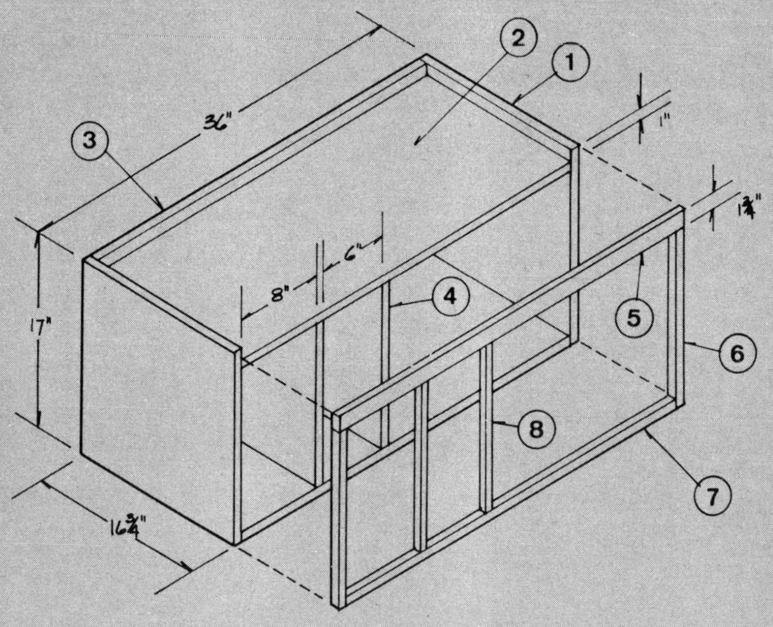


## FIRESIDE BENCH

**Materials List**

(Actual dimensions. See chart page 187.)

| | | |
|---|---|---|
| 1 | 2 pcs. | ¾ x 16¾ x 17 softwood plywood |
| 2 | 2 pcs. | ¾ x 16 x 34½ softwood plywood |
| 3 | 1 pc. | ¾ x 17 x 34½ softwood plywood |
| 4 | 2 pcs. | ¾ x 14½ x 16 softwood plywood |
| 5 | 1 pc. | ¾ x 1¾ x 36 matching lumber |
| 6 | 2 pcs. | ¾ x ¾ x 15¼ matching lumber |
| 7 | 1 pc. | ¾ x ¾ 34½ matching lumber |
| 8 | 2 pcs. | ¾ x ¾ 14½ matching lumber |

# GLASS TOP COFFEE TABLE

This project calls for some careful joinery, but it's well within the scope of anyone who enjoys a showoff piece of craftsmanship. Build it with a good hardwood — maple, birch, or oak for a light tone, walnut for a darker appearance.

Start by cutting the leg pieces and the rails (parts #1 and 2) to size and then carefully lay out the locations for the dowel holes. The holes will be easiest to form if you work on a drill press, but good work can be accomplished with a bit and brace, especially if you work with a doweling jig. It's very important for the holes to be perpendicular to the surfaces they are drilled in.

Next, form the miters on the leg pieces and join parts together with white glue and 6d finishing nails. Now, assemble legs and rails using glue on all mating surfaces and two dowels in each joint. This assembly won't be difficult to do if you have bar clamps or a band clamp. If you lack such equipment, use the tourniquet rope trick; loop strong cord around the assembly and then twist tightly with a strip of wood. Use heavy cardboard under the cord at corners so you don't damage the wood. Allow the glue to dry overnight before removing the clamps.

Final step is to attach the cleats that support the glass. Don't precut these. Instead, start with over-long pieces, trim to size as you install them. Make the attachment with glue and 6d nails.

If you prefer not to have a see-through top, use a piece of ½″ plywood that you can veneer with a plastic laminate of your choice. You can, of course, also use a piece of plywood that matches the wood species used for the table frame.

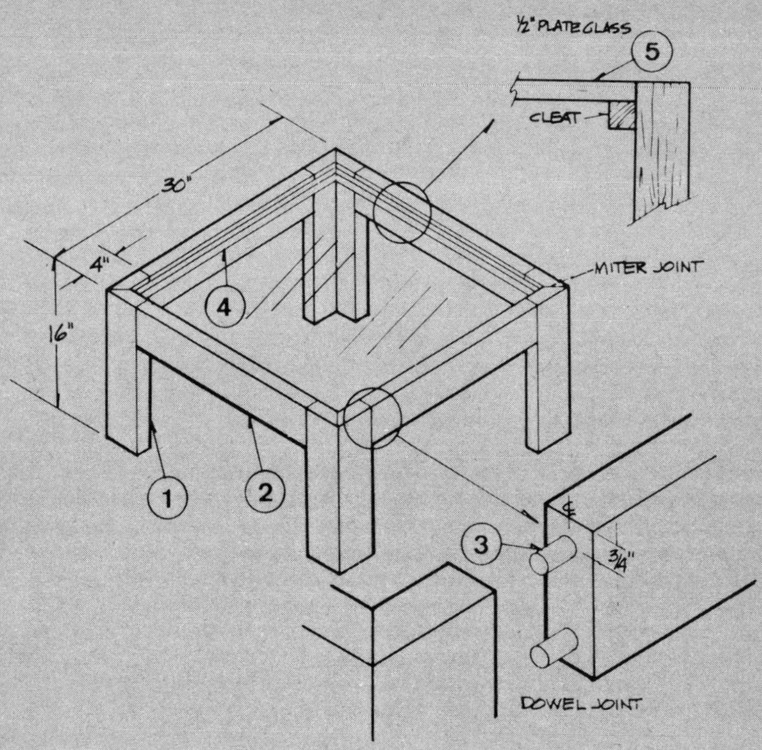


GLASS TOP COFFEE TABLE

**Materials List**

(Actual dimensions. See chart page 187.)

| | | |
|---|---|---|
| 1 | 8 pcs. | 1½ x 4 x 16 lumber |
| 2 | 4 pcs. | 1½ x 4 x 22 lumber |
| 3 | 16 pcs. | ½″ diameter dowel x 2″ long |
| 4 | 4 pcs. | ¾ x ¾ x 27 lumber |
| 5 | 1 pc. | ½ x 27 x 27 plate glass |

# THE CUBE

Basically, this cube is a system of structural boxes, functional and attractive, with almost unlimited use-options. A few units can utilize space in a corner. Two sets of two units each, spanned with a shelf, make a desk. Build enough to cover a wall or to serve as a divider — which way do *you* wish to go?

As the drawings show there are also construction options. Mitered corners reinforced with splines are the most sophisticated approach — not too difficult if power equipment is not available. You can use a less complicated assembly since the units will be stacked and most of the joints will be hidden. Thus, even butt joints may be considered.

Material choices vary — from hardwood plywoods that can be finished clear to paintable types. Painting can be simple — all units the same color — or you can be daring — various units in bright, contrasting tones.

All joints, regardless of design, should be reinforced with white glue and finishing nails. Use 3d or 4d nails for miters, 6d nails for butts.

A unit with a shelf can be used vertically or horizontally, so be sure shelves are centered. The same thinking applies to a unit with a door. Be sure the finger hole is centered between the bottom and top edge of the door and that hinges are placed so the distance from them to the top and bottom of the box is the same. Thus the cubes with doors can be inverted; the door will swing either to the left or the right.

Use a conventional magnetic catch to hold doors in closed position.

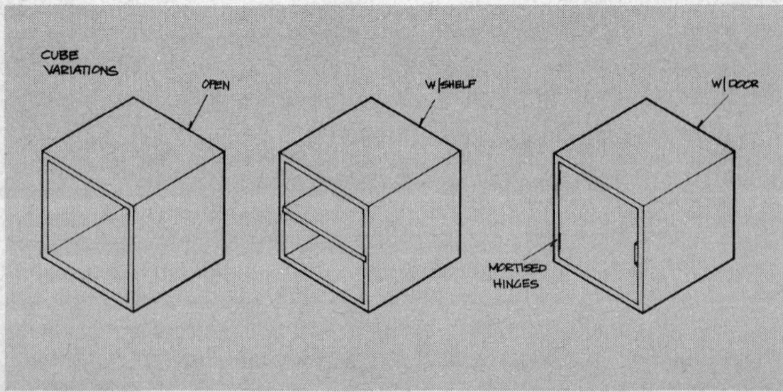

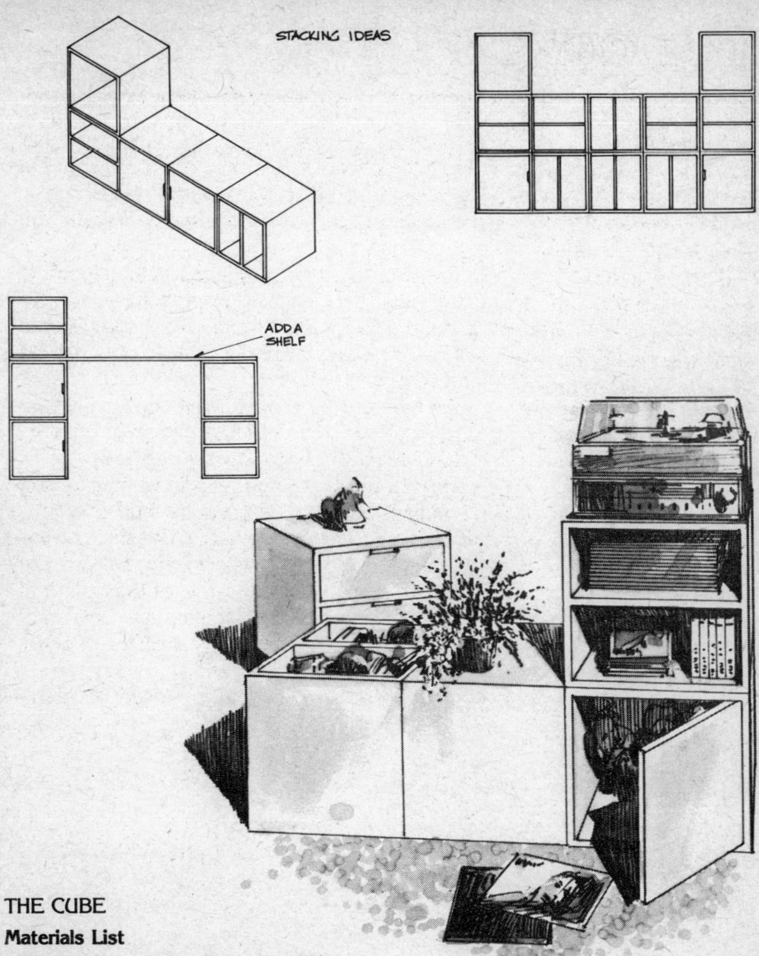


THE CUBE

**Materials List**

(Actual dimensions. See chart page 187.)

Materials list is for a single cube constructed with mitered corners, an inset back, and a door.

| | |
|---|---|
| 4 pcs. | ¾ x 14 x 14 plywood |
| 1 pc. | ¾ x 12½ x 12½ (back) plywood |
| 1 pc. | ¾ x 12½ x 12½ (door) plywood |
| | Note . . . . doors should be "dressed" — that is, reduced a minimum amount in size so they will work without binding. |

# CUSTOM-DESIGNED MAILBOXES

There are many ways to go here — design around ready-made metal boxes that you buy or create from scratch, doing your thing. The postal department doesn't much care about the *size* of the box; it does suggest that the box be waterproof; it demands that box-height be so much above grade and so far from pavement or road. The point is, nothing should interfere with the carrier's need to place or remove mail. The flag too — place it so your postperson can easily reach it. Questions? Easily answered by your carrier or the local post office.

Chances are that one of the designs shown here will meet your needs esthetically and practically.

## MAILBOX #1

Start by cutting the pressure-treated post to correct length and then adding parts #2 and 3 with waterproof glue and 16d nails. Add the bottom of the box with glue and 8d nails driven into the top edge of part #3. Add the sides and then the top. With sides and top, use glue and 8d nails.

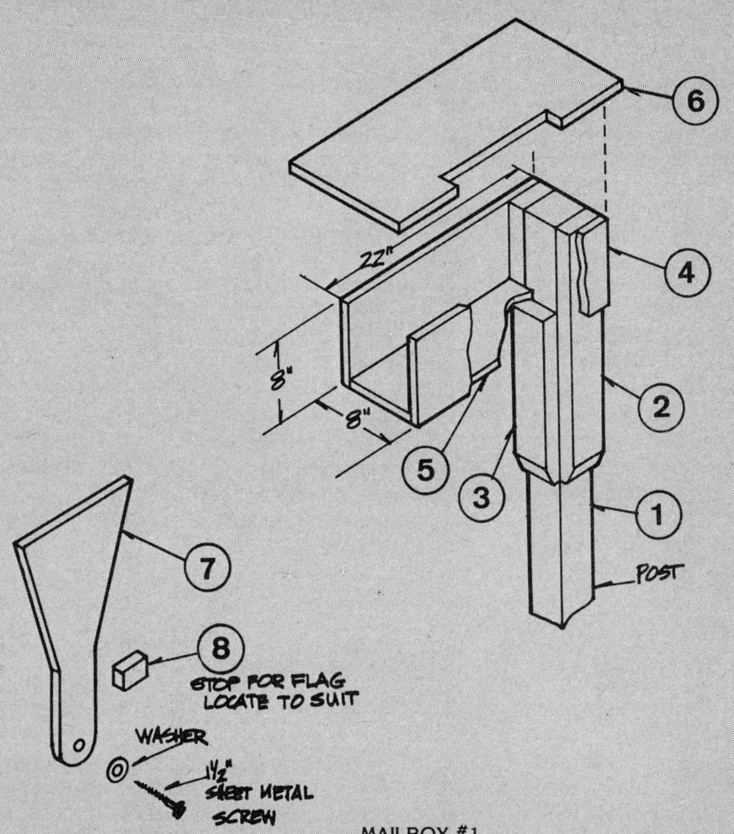


MAILBOX #1

**Materials List**

(Actual dimensions. See chart page 187.)

| | | |
|---|---|---|
| 1 | 1 pc. | 3½ x 3½ x pressure-treated lumber, length to suit |
| 2 | 2 pcs. | 1½ x 3½ x 24 lumber |
| 3 | 1 pc. | 1½ x 3½ x 16 lumber |
| 4 | 2 pcs. | ¾ x 8 x 22 lumber |
| 5 | 1 pc. | ¾ x 6½ x 18½ lumber |
| 6 | 1 pc. | ¾ x 12 x 24 lumber |
| 7 | 1 pc. | ¼ x 3 x 6 lumber |
| 8 | 1 pc. | lumber, size optional |

# MAILBOX #2

Start by cutting the vertical pieces (parts #1 and 2) to correct length. Both parts can be standard 2 x 10 boards (actually 1½" x 9¼"). The front board is used full-width, the back one is ripped to an 8" width. The rabbets in the front board are easy to cut on a table saw or with a portable circular saw. If they are a problem to do, reduce the width of the front board to 8" (to match the back piece) and increase the width of the sides (part #3) by ½". Then both the front and back vertical pieces will attach to the sides with simple butt joints. In either case, attach sides with waterproof glue and 8d nails.

Next step is to add the bottom of the box, using glue and 8d nails that are driven into the top edge of the front piece and through the sides. Finally, add the top, also with glue and 8d nails.

Two holes will be needed to set this project in the ground. Concrete is required in only one of the holes.

In all cases, wood that is buried should be generously treated with a preservative — or the part should be made from pressure-treated wood.

Most of the parts for the mailboxes can be cut from exterior grade plywoods. When the thickness of the part is called out as either ⅜" or ⅝", plywood siding may be substituted.

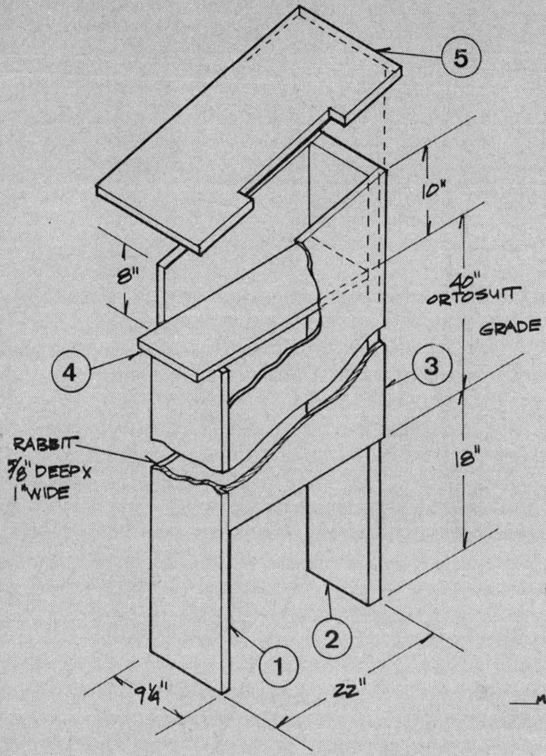

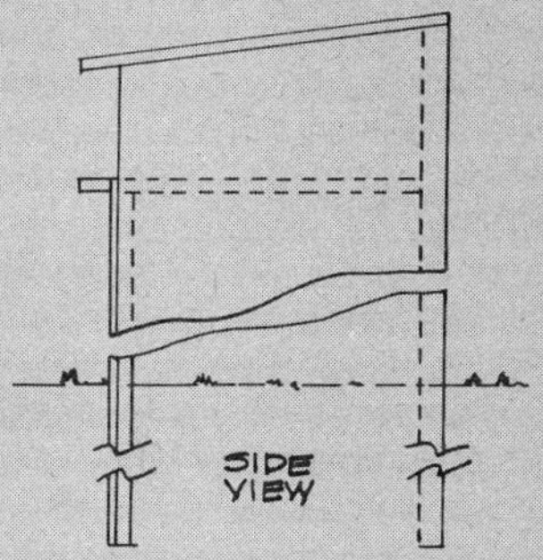

MAILBOX #2

**Materials List**

(Actual dimensions. See chart page 187.)

Dimensions assume the bottom of the box will be 40″ above grade —

| | | |
|---|---|---|
| 1 | 1 pc. | 1½ x 9¼ x 57¼ lumber |
| 2 | 1 pc. | 1½ x 68 lumber |
| 3 | 2 pcs. | ⅝ x 21½ x 50 lumber |
| 4 | 1 pc. | ⅝ x 8 x 22½ lumber |
| 5 | 1 pc. | ⅝ x 13¼ x 24 lumber |

Flag design for *Mailbox #1* also applies for this project.

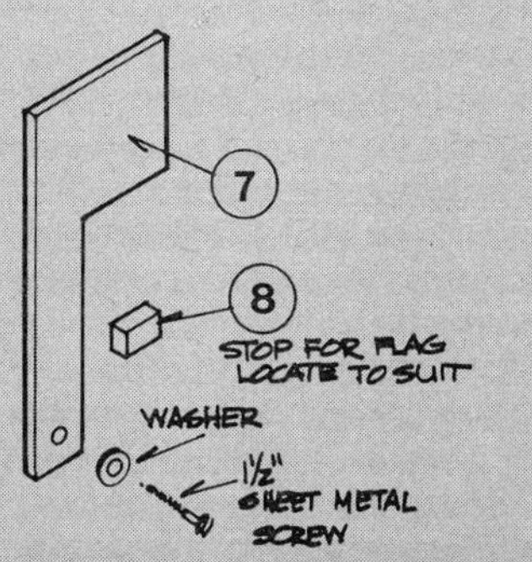

# DOGHOUSE

Start doghouse by assembling the platform (parts 1 and 2) with waterproof glue and galvanized 8d box nails. Next, cut the front and the back. The total height of the front from peak to bottom is 28″; the back is 29½″ high. Form the opening in the front with either a saber saw or a keyhole saw. Be sure to thoroughly sand the sawed edges. Attach the back with glue and 6d nails. The bottom edge of the back lines up with the bottom surface of the deck piece.

Cut the two sides to length (36″) and then determine correct height by checking the parts on what you have assembled so far. The top edge of the sides is cut to match the angle of the roof line.

Cut the two runners (part 6) and assemble them to the sides with glue and 4d nails. Be sure to set these pieces carefully — 1¾″ up from the bottom of the sides and ¾″ in from the back. Add the sides to the assembly with glue and 6d nails.

Now you can add the front, being sure its bottom edge lines up with the bottom edge of the runners. This will leave a 1″ gap over the deck for the pull-out floor.

Cut the roof pieces to size and put them in place with glue and 6d nails. The ridge cover is shaped from a length of 2x4 (actual size = 1½″ x 3½″), and it is attached only with glue.

Final step is to cut the pull-out floor to size and to bore the finger hole which makes it easy to remove the floor for cleaning. Be sure the floor slides in and out easily. Attach the indoor/outdoor carpeting to the floor with standard double-sided carpet tape so replacement, when necessary, will be an easy chore.

Doghouse

**Materials List**

(Actual dimensions. See chart page 187.)

| | | |
|---|---|---|
| 1 | 2 pcs. | 1½ x 3½ x 60 lumber (treated) |
| 2 | 1 pc. | ¾ x 30 x 60 exterior plywood |
| 3 | 1 pc. | ¾ x 29½ x 30 exterior plywood |
| 4 | 2 pcs. | ¾ x 28 x 30 exterior plywood |
| 5 | 2 pcs. | ¾ x 24 x 36 exterior plywood |
| 6 | 2 pcs. | ¾ x 2½ x 30 lumber |
| 7 | 2 pcs. | ¾ x 22 x36 exterior plywood |
| 8 | 1 pc. | 1½ x 3½ x 36 lumber |
| 9 | 1 pc. | ¾ x 30 x 30¾ exterior plywood |

Note . . . the pull-out floor is covered with a 30 x 30¾ piece of indoor/outdoor carpet.

Note . . . the 24″ dimension on part #5 is oversize so it can be checked and trimmed on assembly.

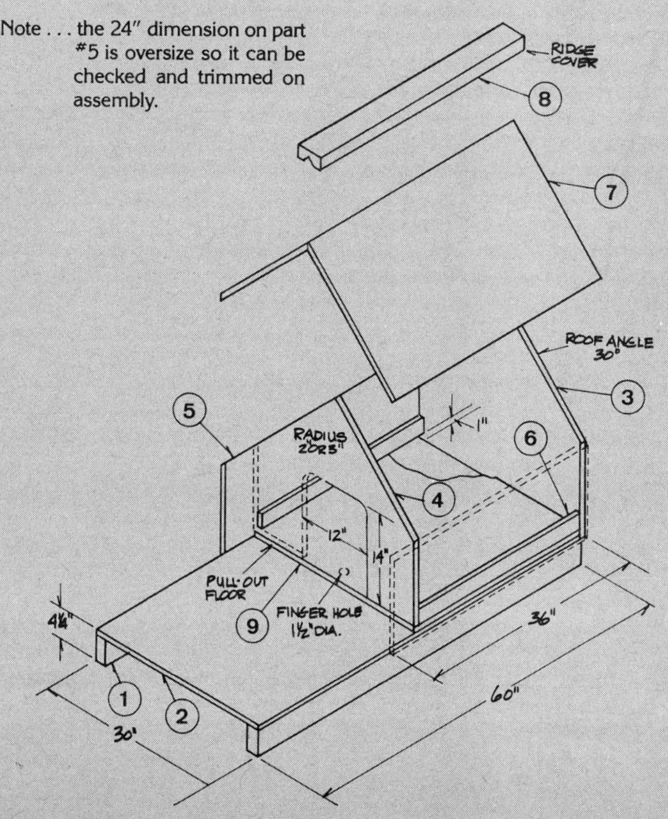

# WINE RACK

There is a correct way to store wine bottles. Essentially, the bottles should be separated, and they should be tipped so the liquid covers the cork. This project provides answers and, while simple, is attractive enough so you can display your collection if you wish.

There are two ways to go when making the shelves for the bottles. One — cut parts to the sizes called for in the materials list and then make the semicircular cutouts by working with a coping saw or saber saw. Two — follow the suggestions shown in the detail drawing. Correct-size holes are formed on the centerline of a full width board, and then the board is sliced in half to end up as two identical pieces. The latter method is better to do if you have a drill press. The large holes, for example, must be done with a fly cutter, an item not usable in a portable drill or hand drill.

Once these parts are made, they are attached to the shelf board (part #3) with glue and 6d finishing nails.

Next, cut the sides of the case and then assemble shelves and sides with glue and 8d finishing nails. Be sure to maintain the 15 degree slope angle of the shelves and the 4″ spacing between them.

Final step is to add the top, securing it with glue and 8d finishing nails. The project is freestanding; that is, you can place it against a wall, on a table, or on a sideboard. You can hang it on a wall if you add a ¼″ plywood back. Drive #10 x 2″ flat head wood screws through the back into wall studs.

## WINE RACK

**Materials List**

(Actual dimensions. See chart page 187.)

| | | |
|---|---|---|
| 1 | 4 pcs. | ¾ x 3½ x 22 lumber |
| 2 | 4 pcs. | ¾ x 3 x 22 lumber |
| 3 | 4 pcs. | ¾ x 8 x 22 lumber |
| 4 | 2 pcs. | ¾ x 11¼ x 23½ lumber |
| 5 | 1 pc. | ¾ x 11¼ x 23½ lumber |

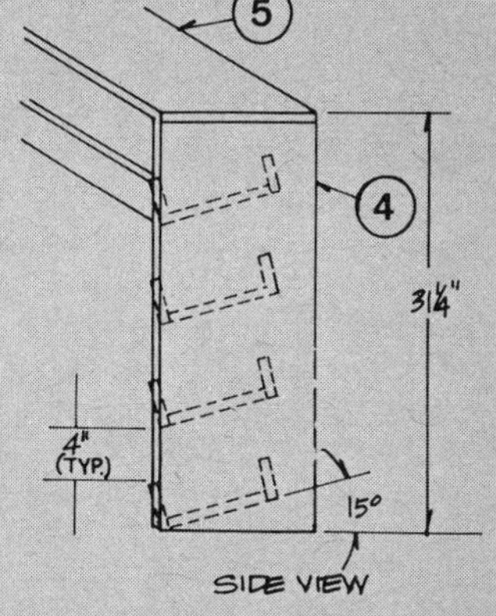


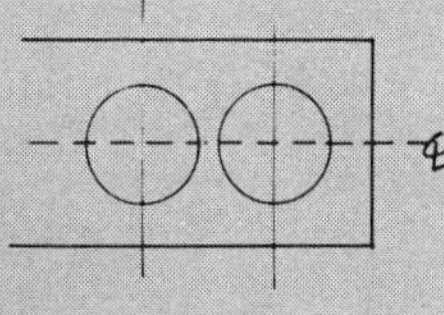


BACK PART OF SHELF
FORM HOLES ON CENTER OF 6" BOARD, THEN CUT ON CENTERLINE

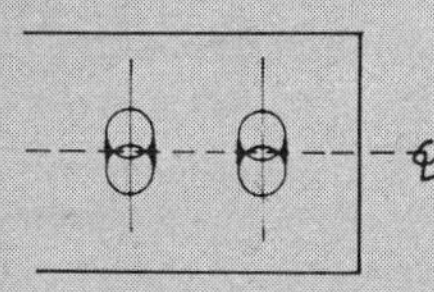


FRONT PART OF SHELF
FORM HOLES AS SHOWN ON 7" BOARD
CUT ON CENTER LINE
CLEAN OUT SHADED AREAS

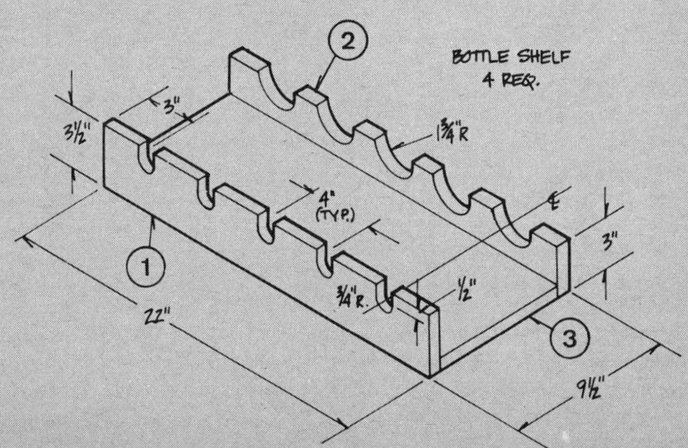

# A BASIC WORKBENCH

By basic we mean an unadorned unit that is easy to make and as sturdy and functional as a workbench should be. All material, except for the shelf, is construction grade fir or a hard softwood lumber in standard sizes — economical and readily available. The project mostly calls for cutting pieces to length and then doing the assembly work.

Start by assembling the two frames. These consist of parts #1 and 2 which are held together with glue and 16d nails.

Next, cut the legs to length and add them to the frames by using glue and carriage bolts in the positions shown in the drawing. If you wish you can use two carriage bolts per bearing instead of the single one shown. Just be careful not to drill through the nails used in the frame assembly.

Cut the surface boards to length and attach them to the top frame with glue and 16d nails. Start with the rear board and work forward. If clamps are available, use them to hold the boards tightly together as you drive the nails.

An extra (not shown in the drawing) is to top the boards with a sheet of ⅜″ or ¼″ tempered hardboard. This will provide a smooth, replaceable surface if you hold it in place with small nails only.

Final step is to add the ¾″ plywood shelf, securing it with glue and 7d nails. A good finish can be applied by brushing two coats of sealer, allowing for drying time and doing a sanding job between coats.

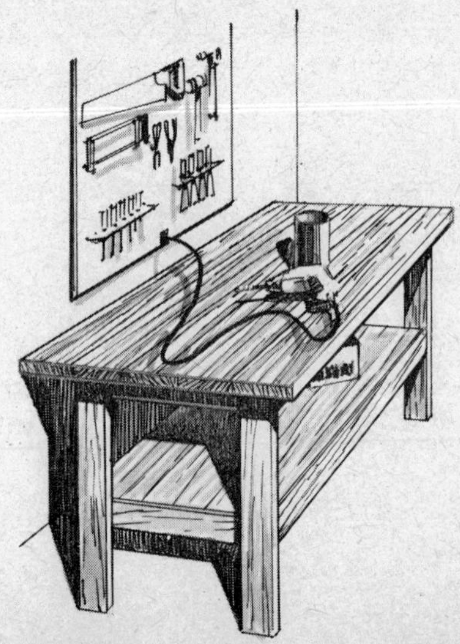

## A BASIC WORKBENCH

**Materials List**

(Actual dimensions. See chart page 187.)

| | | |
|---|---|---|
| 1 | 10 pcs. | 1½ x 3½ x 21½ fir lumber |
| 2 | 4 pcs. | 1½ x 3½ x 54 fir lumber |
| 3 | 4 pcs. | 1½ x 3½ x 32½ fir lumber |
| 4 | 5 pcs. | 1½ x 5½ x 60 fir lumber |
| 5 | 1 pc. | ¾ x 24½ x 54 plywood |

8, ¼″ x 3½″ carriage bolts
with washers and nuts

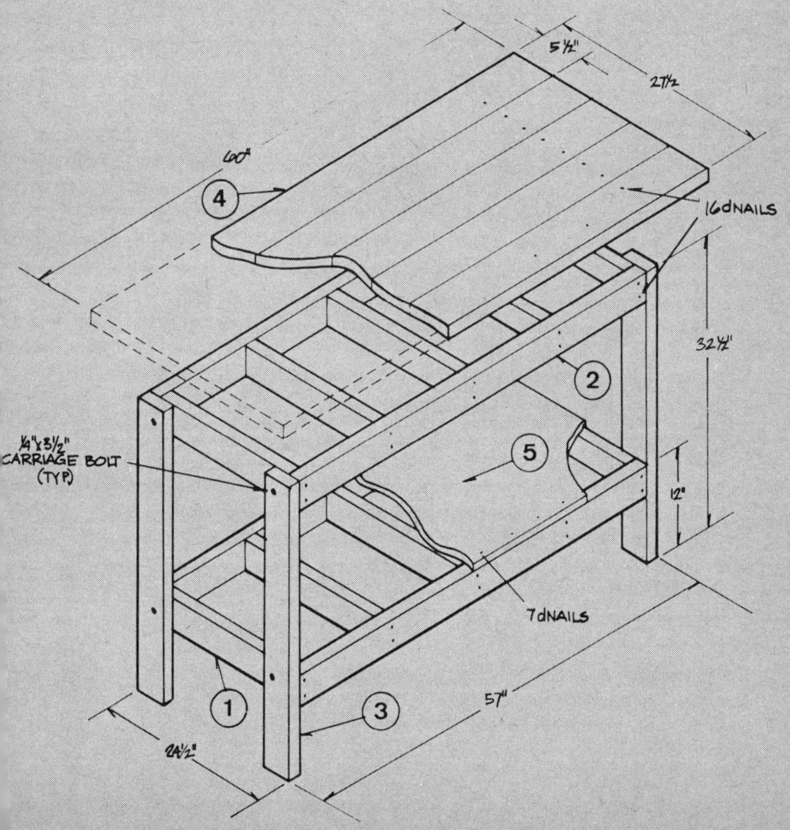

# OUTDOOR PLANTERS

There are probably as many shapes and sizes of planters (or containers) — commercial and homemade — as there are species of flowers and vegetables, but they all have particular traits in common. They must contain soil so a plant can grow; should be sturdy enough and so constructed that they will hold up outdoors; should be tight enough so excess moisture will seep through drainage holes and not through joints; should be made so the wood will be protected from soil contact hazards.

Some woods have a degree of natural immunity against rot and insect damage, among them redwood and cedar, but any wood can be protected. Two common procedures are: line the inside of the planter with sheet plastic; paint soil contact areas with asphaltum. The craftsperson isn't limited to a few wood species, but can choose from materials readily available or for an effect that suits a particular environment. Exterior surfaces of planters can be clear finished, just sealed, left alone to weather, or painted. There are many options.

The construction of planters deserves as much attention as any project. The one that is literally a box with nailed butt joints will soon fall apart. Its durability can be drastically improved merely by adding a *waterproof* glue — not a *water resistant* glue — in the joints. For the best job, make all cuts carefully, use the right glue, reinforce with the fasteners called for, then, as added precaution, seal the inside joint lines with a caulking compound.

Good drainage is important. For one thing, excess moisture will damage the plant. To provide for drainage, drill ⅜″ or ½″ holes through the bottom of the planter. Holes spaced 5″ to 6″ apart will do. Cover the holes with small pieces of aluminum or copper insect screen so soil won't fall through the bottom of the planter. If a plastic liner is used, drill the holes before placing the liner. Then slit the plastic over each hole before placing the screening.

Another precaution — place a layer of small stones in the bottom of the planter before filling with soil. This provides a collection point for water so excess can easily flow through the drainage holes. Don't completely fill planters. Allow for about 1″ of space from the top of the soil to the top of the planter. This makes it easier to water and prevents soil from spilling over.

When choosing a wood, don't neglect to check out the many types of exterior plywood sidings that are available: smooth surfaces, rough-sawn textures, some with grooves; cedar, fir. There are many choices that are both practical and attractive.

TIERED PLANTER

**Materials List**

(Actual dimensions. See chart page 187.)

| | | |
|---|---|---|
| 1 | 4 pcs. | 1½ x 6 x 24 lumber |
| 2 | 1 pc. | ⅝ x 22½ x 22½ lumber |
| 3 | 4 pcs. | 1½ x 10 x 14 lumber |
| 4 | 4 pcs. | ⅝ x 4 x 4 lumber |

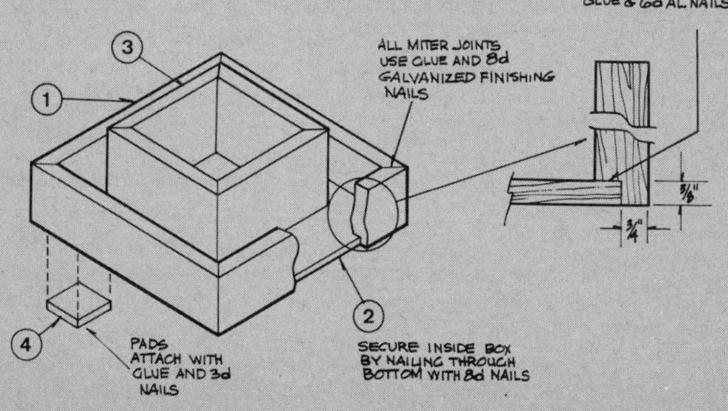

# SKYSCRAPER PLANTER

**Materials List**

(Actual dimensions. See chart page 187.)

| | | A |
|---|---|---|
| 1 | 4 pcs. | ¾ x 10 x 12 exterior plywood |
| 2 | 4 pcs. | 1 x 1 x 12 heart-grade redwood or cedar |
| 3 | 1 pc. | ¾ x 8½ x 8½ exterior plywood |
| | | **B** |
| 1 | 4 pcs. | ¾ x 10 x 16 exterior plywood |
| 2 | 4 pcs. | 1 x 1 x 16 heart-grade redwood or cedar |
| 3 | 1 pc. | ¾ x 8½ x 8½ exterior plywood |
| | | **C** |
| 1 | 4 pcs. | ¾ x 10 x 20 exterior plywood |
| 2 | 4 pcs. | 1 x 1 x 20 heart-grade redwood or cedar |
| 3 | 1 pc. | ¾ x 8½ x 8½ exterior plywood |

GLUE AND 4d GALVANIZED FINISHING NAILS ALL JOINTS

CORNERS OF BOTTOM NOTCHED TO FIT CORNER BLOCKS

CONTAINERS EFFECTIVE WHEN USED IN GROUPS

SEE MATERIALS LIST FOR SIZES OF PARTS

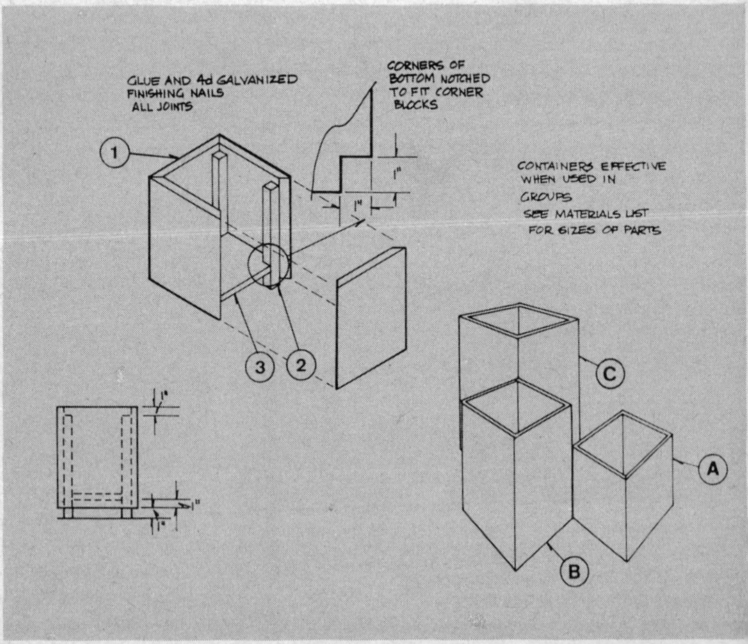

# LARGE PLANTER

**Materials List**

(Actual dimensions. See chart page 187.)

| | | |
|---|---|---|
| 1 | 4 pcs. | 3½ x 3½ x 18 lumber |
| 2 | 2 pcs. | ⅝ x 18 x 24 exterior plywood |
| 3 | 2 pcs. | ⅝ x 16 x 18 exterior plywood |
| 4 | | 1½ x 16 x 22¾ lumber (make from two pieces of 2 x 10 stock) |
| 5 | 2 pcs. | ⅝ x 2½ x 27¾ lumber |
| 6 | 2 pcs. | ⅝ x 2½ x 21 lumber |

Notes . . . cut parts #5 and 6 longer than necessary, trim to size.
⅝″ material = exterior plywood siding.
Attach four swivel type plate casters with 1½ round head wood screws.

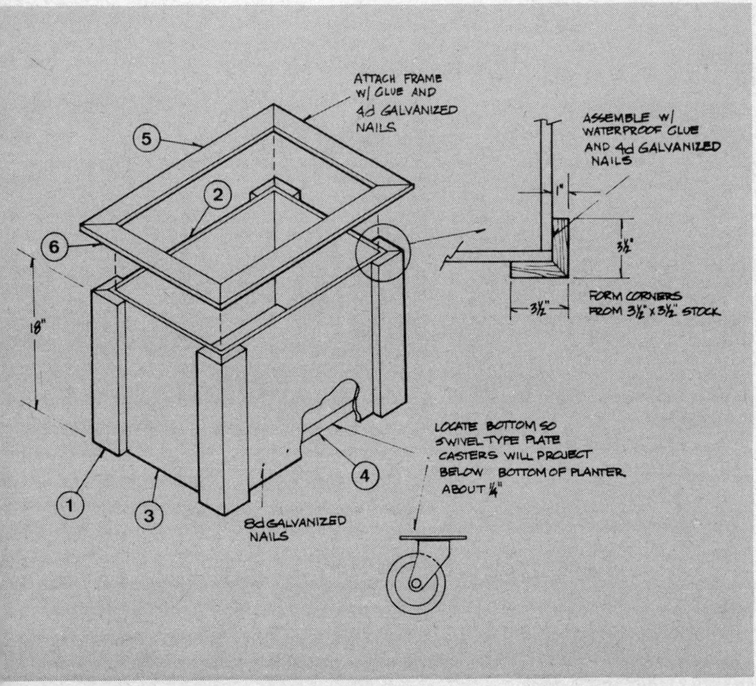

ATTACH FRAME W/ GLUE AND 4d GALVANIZED NAILS
5
2
6
18"
1
3
4
8d GALVANIZED NAILS
ASSEMBLE W/ WATERPROOF GLUE AND 4d GALVANIZED NAILS
1"
3½"
3½"
FORM CORNERS FROM 3½" x 3½" STOCK
LOCATE BOTTOM SO SWIVEL TYPE PLATE CASTERS WILL PROJECT BELOW BOTTOM OF PLANTER ABOUT ¼"

# PATIO TABLE and BENCHES

You have a patio, and it's a great place to lounge; but then comes the idea of outdoor dining, so you need a table and seats. Our projects serve nicely: attractive and sturdy and designed for a minimum of construction procedures. The most you have to do is saw standard-width boards to correct length and drill a few holes.

Start by cutting the rails and the legs for the table to length. Assemble the legs to the top rails by using waterproof glue and the carriage bolts called for. Be sure the legs are set 90 degrees to the rails, then add the bottom rail.

The stretcher (part #3) can be done as shown in the drawing — it adds a touch — or you can simply butt it between the rails like the bench stretcher. Doing the dadoes with power equipment is easy; with hand tools, make outline saw cuts first and then clean away the waste with a chisel.

Add the table-top boards after you have coated the upper edges of the top rails with waterproof glue. Drive the brass screws so they hit the centerline of the outboard rail. Use a piece of ¼″ plywood as a gauge for correct spacing between the boards.

Follow the same construction procedures when assembling the benches.

Projects like this are often done with kiln-dried or construction grades of redwood — much depends on the effect desired and money to be spent. But don't ignore other woods like pine, fir, and cedar. They do well outdoors if treated with an exterior type sealer for a natural look or if they are painted

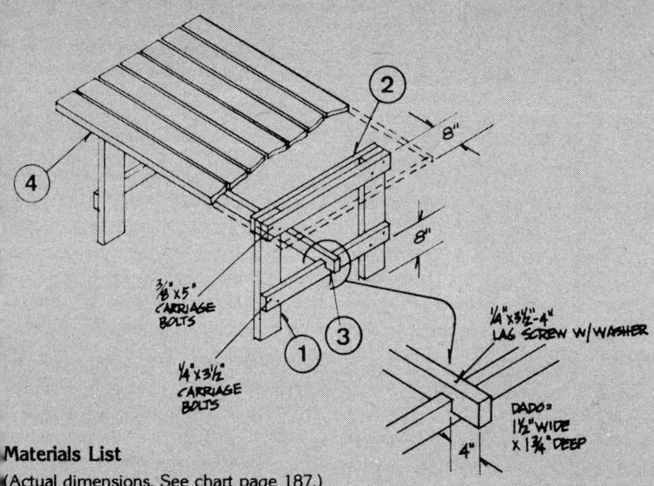


## Materials List

(Actual dimensions. See chart page 187.)

TABLE

| | | |
|---|---|---|
| 1 | 4 pcs. | 1½ x 5½ x 27½ lumber |
| 2 | 6 pcs. | 1½ x 3½ x 34 lumber |
| 3 | 1 pc. | 1½ x 3½ x 58 lumber |
| 4 | 7 pcs. | 1½ x 5½ x 66 lumber |
| | 8 | ⅜″ x 5″ carriage bolts |
| | 8 | ¼″ x 3½″ carriage bolts |
| | 2 | ¼″ x 3½″ · 4″ lag screws |
| | 28 | #16 x 3 ″ brass flat head wood screws |

4
8"
2
1/4"x5"
CARRIAGE
BOLTS
1
3
1/4"x3 1/2"
CARRIAGE
BOLTS
6"
16d
GAL. NAILS

TWO BENCHES

| | |
|---|---|
| 8 pcs. | 1½ x 3½ x 16½ lumber |
| 12 pcs. | 1½ x 3½ x 11¼ lumber |
| 2 pcs. | 1½ x 3½ x 47 lumber |
| 4 pcs. | 1½ x 5½ x 66 lumber |
| 16 | ¼″ x 5″ carriage bolts |
| 16 | ¼″ x 3½″ carriage bolts |
| 8 | 16d nails |
| 16 | #16 x 3″ brass flat head wood screws |

All hardware (except for brass screws) should be galvanized.

OVERALL SIZES

TABLE = 29" HIGH
40" WIDE
66" LONG
BENCH 18" HIGH
11¼" WIDE
66" LONG

# CHILD'S DESK

All parts of this project are ¾" hardwood plywood except for the leg assemblies, which are lumber. If you prefer a lighter appearance, substitute 2 x 3 stock (actually 1½" x 2½") for the leg parts. If so, change the dimensions of the mortise to ½" wide x 1½" long x 1½" deep.

Start work by cutting all parts of the top structure to size. Form the dadoes required in the two end pieces and then assemble the bottom, back, and ends using butt joints reinforced with glue and 6d finishing nails.

Next, cut the pieces for the legs and form the mortise-tenon joints that are required. Anyone with a drill press and mortising chisels will not need guidance here, but if you lack power equipment, form the mortise by drilling a series of overlapping ½" holes and then cleaning out the waste with a chisel. Form the tenon by making cuts with a saw, preferably a backsaw. The tenon should be a slip fit, snug but not so tight that you must use a mallet to seat it. Form the top end of the legs with a saw. The shape is essentially a very wide rabbet.

Assemble the mortise-tenon joint with glue and two 3d finishing nails driven from the inside of the base so they penetrate the tenon.

Attach the leg assemblies to the case with glue and by driving #10 x 1¼" flat head wood screws from the inside — two screws into each leg, located so they will not be visible when the writing surface is added. Coat the dadoes with glue and slip the writing surface (part #4) into place; then add the vertical divider.

Use a veneer wood-tape to conceal all exposed plywood edges. Then, if you wish, use a contact cement to attach a sheet of plastic laminate to the writing surface.

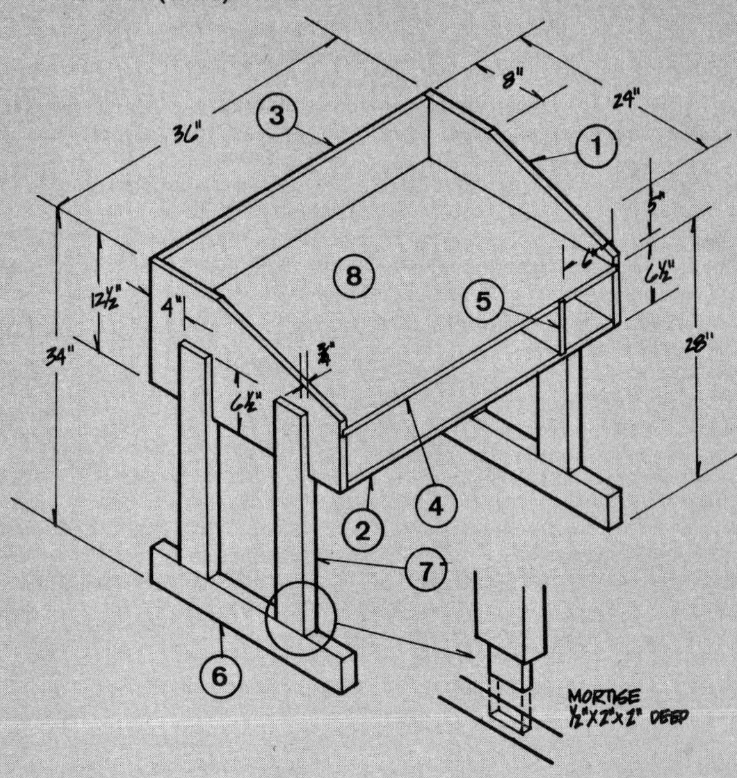


CHILD'S DESK

¾"
ALL DADOES

**Materials List**

(Actual dimensions. See chart page 187.)

| | | |
|---|---|---|
| 1 | 2 pcs. | ¾ x 12½ x 24 hardwood plywood |
| 2 | 1 pc. | ¾ x 23¼ x 34½ hardwood plywood |
| 3 | 1 pc. | ¾ x 12½ x 34½ hardwood plywood |
| 4 | 1 pc. | ¾ x 23¼ x 35¼ hardwood plywood |
| 5 | 1 pc. | ¾ x 5¾ x 23¼ hardwood plywood |
| 6 | 2 pcs. | 1½ x 3½ x 24 matching lumber |
| 7 | 4 pcs. | 1½ x 3½ x 26½ matching lumber (includes length required for tenon) |
| 8 | 1 pc. | (optional) 23¼ x 34½ — plastic laminate |

# Great Possibilities for your home

The following 16 pages contain colorful ideas using Georgia-Pacific products as the finishing touch on your dream project. We know you'll be inspired when you see the look high-quality materials give a home. If you'd like more information or more ideas, your G-P Registered Building Materials Dealer has a full line of products, literature, and samples to help you get started.

**Barnplank™ paneling**, below, is the perfect choice for those who love the sturdy, weatherworn look of authentic barnboards. Barnplank's real Ponderosa pine face veneer comes in Weathered White (shown), Weathered Brown, and Weathered Gray.

Pine veneered plywood 5/16″

# PANELING

**For luxurious surroundings,** treat yourself to **Design VIII™ Mural Pecan** paneling, upper right. Real hardwood face veneer and eight-inch planking give an elegant effect. **Bridgeport® Lantern Pine,** lower right, offers a brightening touch and an easy-care finish. **Spectrum® White Pecan,** below, livens up this kitchen at a very low cost. All of these panelings are available in a variety of shades.

Simulated woodgrain finish plywood 5/32″ or 5.2 mm

Pecan veneered plywood ¼″

Pine veneered plywood ¼″

Birch veneered plywood ¼″

Pine veneered plywood ¼″

**Chateau II™ Knotty Birch**, opposite, imparts a mellow beauty to any room. Here it is used as vertical wainscoting and horizontal wallcovering. **Ol' Savannah® Chandler's Pine**, left, creates the feeling of well-worn pine boards. The mood is one of relaxation and hospitality. **Cedarglen™ paneling** in Riverock Gray, below, is one of the new selection of subtle cedar grain prints. Available in three lovely neutral shades.

Simulated woodgrain plywood ¼″

**A warm, traditional atmosphere** is created by **Old World® Knotty Cedar,** opposite. It is a plywood paneling with a wood face veneer embossed with distressing and "tick marks." Oak, ash, and pecan woodgrain prints alternate in six random planks per panel in **Harmonic III™,** right. The panels have a realistic textured look with a durable gloss finish. **Townhall® Esplanade,** below, features a distinctively printed face veneer.

Simulated woodgrain finish plywood 5/32″

Simulated woodgrain finish plywood 5/32″ or 5.2 mm

Cedar veneered plywood ¼″

# SIDING

**Redwood siding,** near right, provides the natural warmth and beauty of fine wood. **Economical fir plywood siding,** far right, is especially suited to exterior pigment stain. **Teton hardboard siding,** below right, combines the good looks of lumber with the economy and durability of hardboard. **Redwood siding,** below, offers beauty and lasting value.

**Cedar siding,** opposite page, shows with its good looks why wood covers more homes than any other type of siding. **Teton,** left, is available in four rich earth tones. It is suitable for single- and multi-story construction because the panels are stackable. This attractive sapwood-streaked **clear grade redwood siding,** below, is only one of the available grades of redwood.

**Unique designs** are easily achieved with the versatility of **redwood lumber siding,** right. Redwood is particularly suitable as the siding on this facade. Georgia-Pacific offers **pine plywood siding,** below, with a distinctive grain characteristic in rough-sawn reverse board-and-batten.

# DECKS and FENCES

**Fir plywood siding**, below, is available in rough-sawn or smooth textures. As shown here, it adapts to a modern design; it can also be used for a traditional look.

**Stained cedar fence**, opposite, is made of one of the most durable of building materials. Cedar responds beautifully to heavy-bodied and transparent stains. The sumptuous **hot tub and deck** combination, opposite right, lends itself perfectly to redwood. **Treated Douglas fir**, opposite below, will ensure the long life and weatherability of a deck. **The redwood of the deck**, left, has natural weather-resistant properties. **Redwood also blends** very well with other materials like brick, as in the deck, below. Of course, few things harmonize better with nature than redwood.

He's your Georgia-Pacific Registered Dealer. And he can help you get "oohs and ahhs" on all kinds of do-it-yourself projects. From building a bookcase or finishing a rec room to paneling your bedroom, or even adding on a whole new room.

So, when you're ready to build a project from this book, see your G-P Registered Dealer.

Redi-Cuts

Nails

eorgia·Pacific
GP
REGISTERED DEALER
Home of quality building products and service

# BUTCHERBLOCK TABLE

Functional and sturdy, it's a lot more than the conventional light-duty cutting board. Professional blocks are usually maple or birch, and you can opt for such material or choose easier-to-work, more economical pine; straight grain fir is handsome and tough. Whichever you choose, the material must be clear and kiln-dried.

Cut all parts to the sizes shown in the materials list and then do careful layouts to mark the locations of holes for the threaded rod and for the dadoes required in the legs and in the two rails. Drill holes a bit oversize (about 9/16″) so rods will be easy to insert and to provide some leeway for aligning the slab parts.

The two end pieces are counterbored so washers and nuts can be set below the surface of the wood. The diameter of the counterbore can be judged by the size of the washer; its depth depends on whether you wish to conceal the fasteners with wood plugs. Either way, be sure to form the counterbore before you drill the through hole.

Dadoes can be formed with power equipment by using a dado assembly, or by hand by first making outline cuts with a backsaw and then cleaning out the waste with a chisel. All detail work is accomplished before assembly begins. Test for accuracy by putting parts together without glue.

Final step is to coat mating surfaces with glue as they are assembled. Use a glue with a long set time, like Liquid Hide glue, since it allows more time for placing parts. Start by inserting rods through one end slab-piece; add others after coating them with glue. Be sure to insert the legs in correct positions. Take up on the nuts a bit at a time, making sure that all parts are flush with each other. Check the legs with a square; they must be perpendicular to the slab. Remove all excess glue with a damp cloth.

Rails can be added by using only glue. Bar clamps make the job easier but, lacking them, use the old rope trick. Make a loop around the parts that must be pulled together and then use a stick to twist the loop tightly — like a tourniquet.

All parts, except the top, can be stained and varnished or finished clear. Use a good grade of salad oil as a finish for the work surface. Apply it generously, allow it to soak in, then wipe dry with a lint-free cloth. Repeat the treatment periodically.

BUTCHERBLOCK TABLE

**Materials List**

(Actual dimensions. See chart page 187.)

| | | |
|---|---|---|
| 1 | 14 pcs. | 1½ x 3½ x 24 lumber |
| | 2 pcs. | 1½ x 3½ x 17 lumber |
| 2 | 4 pcs. | 1½ x 3½ x 30 lumber |
| 3 | 2 pcs. | 1½ x 3½ x 20 lumber |
| 4 | 1 pc. | 1½ x 3½ x 16½ lumber |
| | 3 pcs. ½" threaded rod, 24" long, with 6 washers and 6 nuts | |

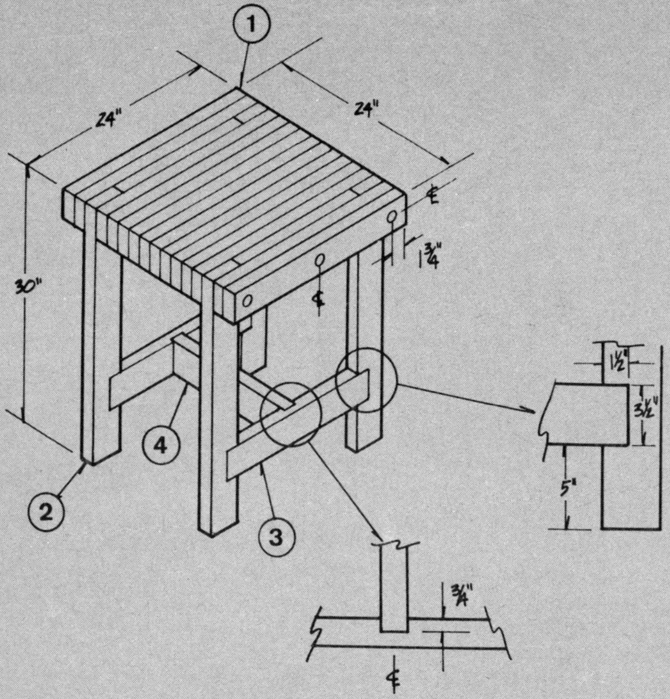

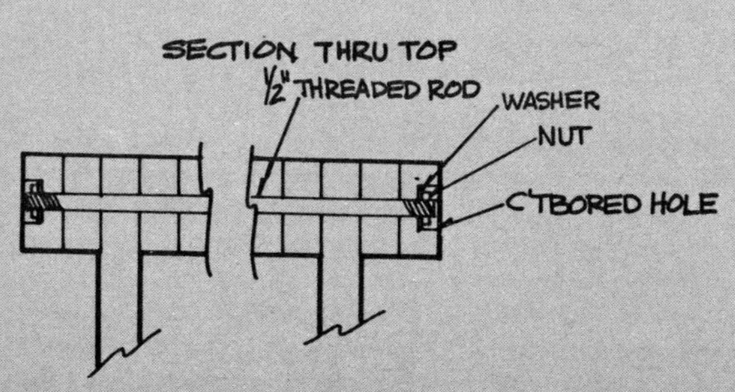

1
24"
24"
30"
℄
1¾"
℄
4
2
3
1½"
3½"
5"
¾"
℄

SECTION THRU TOP

½" THREADED ROD
WASHER
NUT
C'TBORED HOLE

# WORKING HEADBOARD

The headboard provides ample storage space behind the top-side slante doors which also serve as pillow rests for bedtime reading. The outboar extensions are suitable for lamps; the center section will hold readin materials or other small items. The unit is freestanding so placement i flexible, and it's movable when you wish to rearrange things.

Start by cutting the back, front, and the two shelves (parts 1, 2, 3, and 4) t the sizes called for in the materials list. The front and back are dadoed t receive the shelves; the four pieces are assembled with glue and 6 finishing nails.

Next, add the ends and the dividers (#5) and the center shelf (#6 All butt joints here are connected with glue and 8d finishing nails. Add th frames for the end doors, first attaching the vertical pieces and the cutting the horizontal pieces so they will be a snug fit. Secure with glue an 8d finishing nails. Cut the door to fit the frame opening, but allow abo 1/16″ clearance to guard against binding. Cut mortises for the hinges; us a magnetic catch to hold the door shut. Add a pull or drill a 1″ hole s you can use a finger to open the door.

The drawing detail "A" shows how the top piece (#13) is shape and how a strip is added (#14) to the top edge of the front. If you wo with lumber that is wide enough (1x8 which actually measures ¾″ x 7¼′ you will be able to get both pieces by making one saw cut. Add the top pie with glue and 8d nails, the strip with glue and 4d nails. The length the slanted doors is 24″, but measure the assembly before cutting them width. Mortise at the bottom end for hinges.

The ⅜″ x ¾″ strips (numbers 11 and 12) are used to hide exposed p wood edges and are attached with glue and 3d finished nails. Final step is use veneer woodtape to hide other plywood edges. This will occur at t front edge of the center shelf and at part of the ends of the front and ba

## ATERIALS

Use a good grade of plywood — knotty pine, birch, ash, mahogany, alnut — whatever suits your decor. Lumber pieces (numbers 7, 8, 9, 11, 2, 13, 14) should be material that matches the plywood species.

## WORKING HEADBOARD (cont'd)

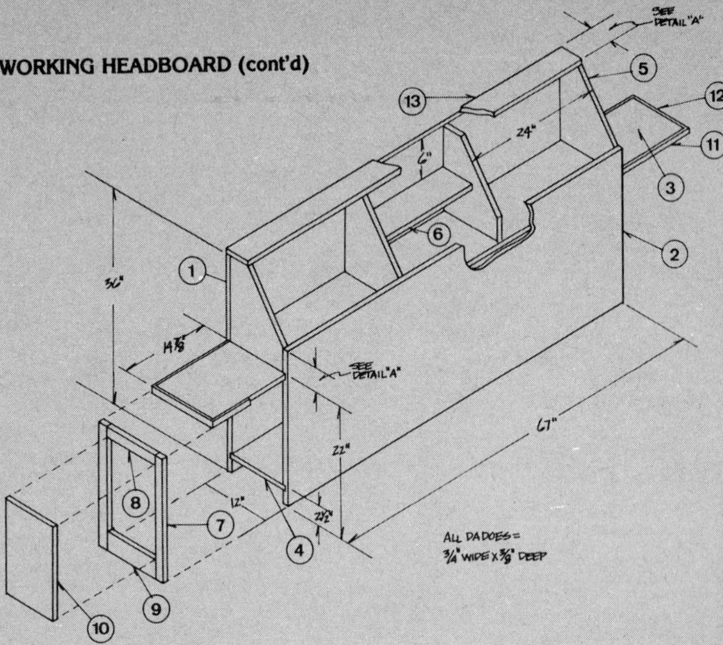

### WORKING HEADBOARD

**Materials List**

(Actual dimensions. See chart page 187.)

| | | |
|---|---|---|
| 1 | 1 pc. | ¾ x 36 x 67 plywood |
| 2 | 1 pc. | ¾ x 26 x 67 plywood |
| 3 | 1 pc. | ¾ x 11¼ x 96 plywood |
| 4 | 1 pc. | ¾ x 11¼ x 67 plywood |
| 5 | 4 pcs. | ¾ x 10½ x 14 plywood |
| 6 | 1 pc. | ¾ x 6 x 19 plywood |
| 7 | 4 pcs. | ¾ x 1½ x 21¼ lumber |
| 8 | 2 pcs. | ¾ x 1½ x 9 lumber |
| 9 | 2 pcs. | ¾ x 2½ x 9 lumber |
| 10 | 2 pcs. | ¾ x 9 x 17¼ plywood |
| 11 | 4 pcs. | ⅜ x ¾ x 14⅞ lumber |
| 12 | 2 pcs. | ⅜ x ¾ x 12 lumber |
| 13 | 1 pc. | ¾ x 5⅛ x 67 lumber |
| 14 | 1 pc. | ¾ x 1 x 67 lumber |
| 15 | 2 pcs. | ¾ x 13 x 24 plywood (13″ dimension is oversize — cut to fit on assembly) |

4 pairs hinges

2 magnetic catches for end doors

DETAIL "A"

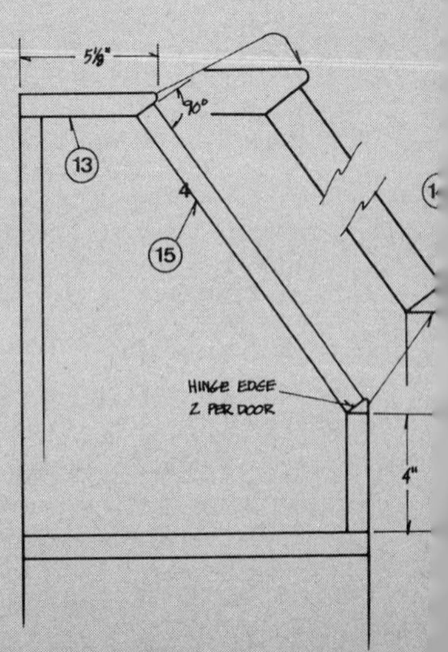

# GARDEN CART

This is a sturdy cart that will hold more than 5 cubic feet of whatever you must transport. Use it to tote leaves, soil, debris, firewood; large wheels let it move easily.

Start the project by assembling the bin, which consists of parts 1, 2, 3, and 4. Best procedure is to assemble the sides to the back, then add the bottom and finally, the front. Use waterproof glue and 8d galvanized box nails for all joints.

Next, shape the axle blocks and attach them to the bin with glue and two ⅜″ x 3″ carriage bolts. Use a flat washer and then a lock washer under the nut. The bushings suggested will be available from a machine shop supply store. If you wish to eliminate them, drill holes through the blocks to suit the axle diameter, but make the blocks of maple or a similar tough wood and coat the hole with grease before placing the axle.

The legs (part #8) will not be difficult to make if you work with aluminum. Steel bars are workable if you have equipment (a torch) to heat the bend areas. Drill holes through the legs and then attach them with ¼″ x 1½″ bolts.

Make the handle (parts 5 and 6) and then attach to the bin with glue and ¼″ x 2″ carriage bolts.

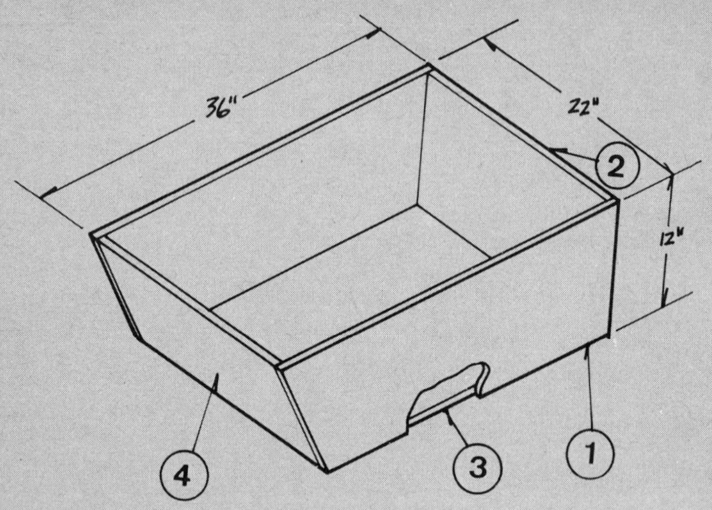


GARDEN CART

**Materials List**

(Actual dimensions. See chart page 187.)

| | | |
|---|---|---|
| 1 | 2 pcs. | ¾ x 12 x 36 exterior plywood |
| 2 | 1 pc. | ¾ x 12 x 20½ exterior plywood |
| 3 | 1 pc. | ¾ x 20½ x 30 exterior plywood |
| 4 | 1 pc. | ¾ x 16 x 20½ exterior plywood |
| 5 | 2 pcs. | ¾ x 2½ x 30 lumber |
| 6 | 1 pc. | 1" diameter dowel x 26" |
| 7 | 2 pcs. | 1½ x 3½ x 6 hardwood |
| 8 | 2 pcs. | ¼ x 1 x 26 aluminum or steel bar stock |
| 9 | 2 pcs. | 16" diameter wheels |
| | 4 | ⅜" x 3" carriage bolts w/flat washer, lock washer and nuts |
| | 4 | ¼" x 2" carriage bolts w/flat washer, lock washer and nuts |

Note . . . inside diameter of bushing to suit outside diameter of axle to be ½" or ⅝" steel rod. The length of part #3 and the height of part #4 are oversize so correct size can be judged on assembly.

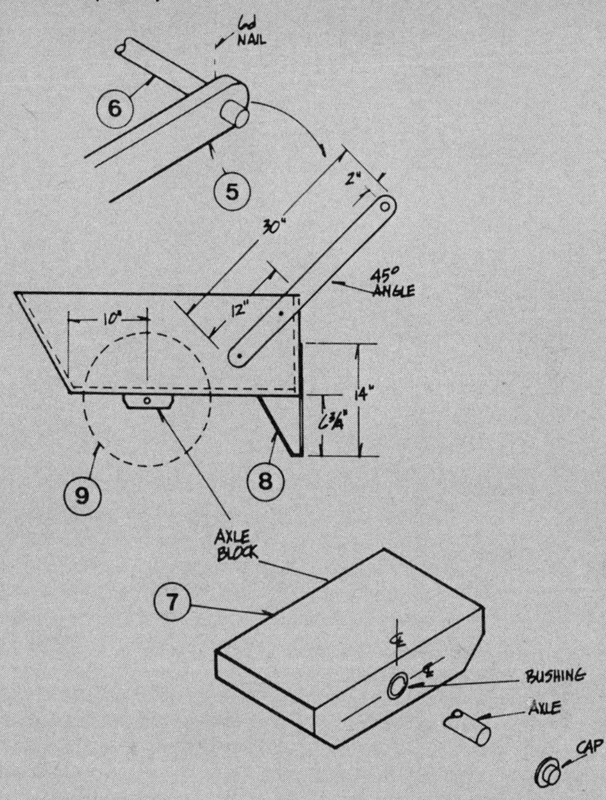


There are various types of wheels to choose: bicycle wheels, wheels for wheelbarrows, wheels for carts. Wheel diameter should not be less than 16", but it can be as much as 20". If the latter, adjust the length of the legs to extend below the bottom of the bin an additional 2".

Use standard ½" or ⅝" diameter steel rod as an axle. Cut the rod to length with a hacksaw after judging its length on assembly. Use conventional caps as hub caps on the axles. These are made so you just tap them on with a hammer to secure them on the axle-ends.

Give all wood parts a coat of exterior grade sealer; leave natural or follow with a paint color of your choice.

# ADJUSTABLE SUN SCREEN

A sun screen can effectively reduce inside temperatures, but since there are times when you might wish to use the sun's heat, an adjustable version makes sense. This one is sized for a 3′ x 4′ window, so changes are required if you build for a window of a different size. If the slats will be much longer, add an intermediate stringer and attach it top-side with a third hinge. Getting even more adjustment than the design provides is just a matter of using a longer brace.

First make the stringers, cutting them to length and then clamping them together so you can make the slat-seat cuts across both. The slats are standard-width lumber (1x3), so all you have to do is cut to length and then attach to the stringers with waterproof glue and 7d nails.

The next step is to attach the supports, securing them to the house wall, preferably into studs, with lag screws. Make and attach the adjustment brace after the strap hinges have been installed. The position and the length of the brace does not have to abide by what is shown in the drawing. Actually, it's best to judge its placement after studying the sun's travel around your own home.

There are various ways to make the slot in the brace — on a drill press with a router bit, with a portable router, with a coping saw or a saber saw — what equipment do you have?

Redwood is a good material for this project, but other species like pine or fir are okay, especially if you plan a paint finish.

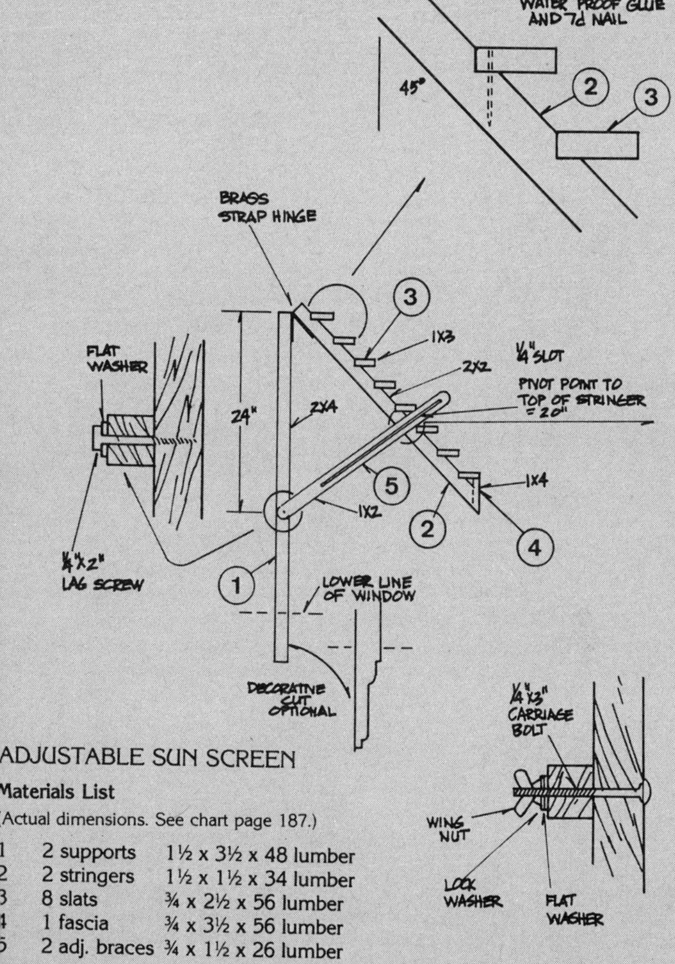


# ADJUSTABLE SUN SCREEN

## Materials List

(Actual dimensions. See chart page 187.)

| | | |
|---|---|---|
| 1 | 2 supports | 1½ x 3½ x 48 lumber |
| 2 | 2 stringers | 1½ x 1½ x 34 lumber |
| 3 | 8 slats | ¾ x 2½ x 56 lumber |
| 4 | 1 fascia | ¾ x 3½ x 56 lumber |
| 5 | 2 adj. braces | ¾ x 1½ x 26 lumber |

one pair 4″ or 5″ brass strap hinges
2 ¼″ x 2″ lag screws w/washer
2 ¼″ x 3″ carriage bolts w/flat washer, lock washer and wing nut

# A VERY BASIC DISPLAY SHELF

There are as many ways to build shelves as there are items that can be stored on them. And there are few areas in a home that can't be made more useable or more attractive through the use of shelving. Shelves can be pretty or not, but they must always be practical. The installation area and the purpose of the shelves should be important guides. An easy-to-do storage shelf in a garage for storing paint cans and such can simply be readymade metal brackets that you screw to studs to hold a board, but it would not do in an area where books, a treasured vase, stereo equipment, and so on are part of the decor.

To a great extent, what you will place on the shelves will determine the spacing between shelves and even the type of material you should use. Average books can be stored on shelves that are spaced 9″ to 10″ but there are those coffee-table volumes that need more height. So, allowing for off-sizes at the start — by varying shelf spacing or by including a two-shelf-high nook — is a good idea.

A few books aren't heavy, but a 10-foot row has considerable weight; so decide beforehand whether to use 2″ stock (for extra strength over long spans) or to work with 1″ boards and provide needed support by including vertical dividers between shelves.

The depth of shelves should not be arbitrary. Narrow shelves that do the job are better than excessively wide ones since they take up less space, are cheaper to install, and minimize areas that must be dusted. Often, shelves of various widths provide the answer to a problem. If so, use the wider shelves at bottom areas of the project.

Lumber and plywood are the most popular materials for shelf projects regardless of whether the shelves are a built-in type or merely spanning readymade brackets. Lumber can be purchased in ready-to-use sizes. For example, a 1 x 10 board, which actually measures ¾″ x 9½″, is about right for average books. The advantage of plywood is that you can rip it to whatever width needed. Its disadvantage is exposed edges, but the problem is easily solved. Cover the edges with strips of wood-veneer banding, or with thin strips of wood that you glue and nail in place, or even with an attractive moulding. Be sure unit is attached to wall studs with screws and lag bolts.

Try to anticipate future needs when you install non-adjustable, built-in shelving. More shelf space than you need right now is better than too little tomorrow.

Many types of perforated strips with matching shelf-support brackets are available. The strips are attached with screws to walls — preferably into studs — the brackets lock into the strips. With careful planning you can avoid the prosaic parallel-shelf look. Screws used to attach the strips should penetrate the studs a minimum of 1″. Use longer screws if the shelves must support heavy objects.

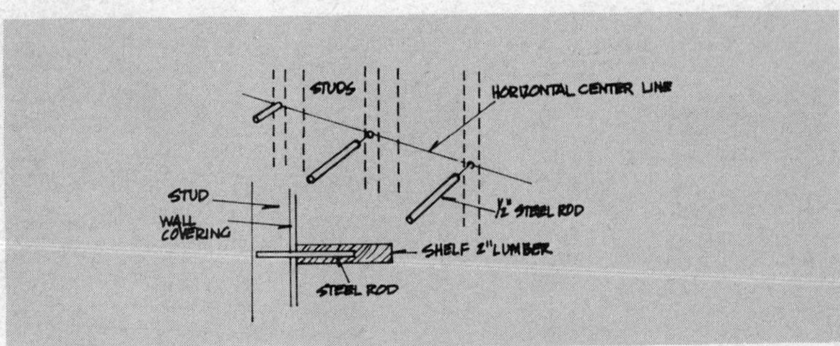


Shelves installed as shown above appear to float since they have no visible means of support. The job does call for careful drilling, but it's really a fast way to get shelves up, and the result is attractive and interesting.

Use a level to draw horizontal lines on the wall at shelf heights. Locate the center of a wall stud, then mark across the line at 16″ intervals. Drill ½″ holes 3″ deep into each stud. Hold the shelf against the wall so you can mark its back edge for the mating holes. Holes in the shelf should be about half the shelf width.

Use a hacksaw to cut ½″ steel rod to correct lengths — 3″ plus thickness of wall covering plus half shelf width.

Hammer rods into the wall and then place the shelves.

Use 2″ boards (actually 1½″ thick) as shelf material.

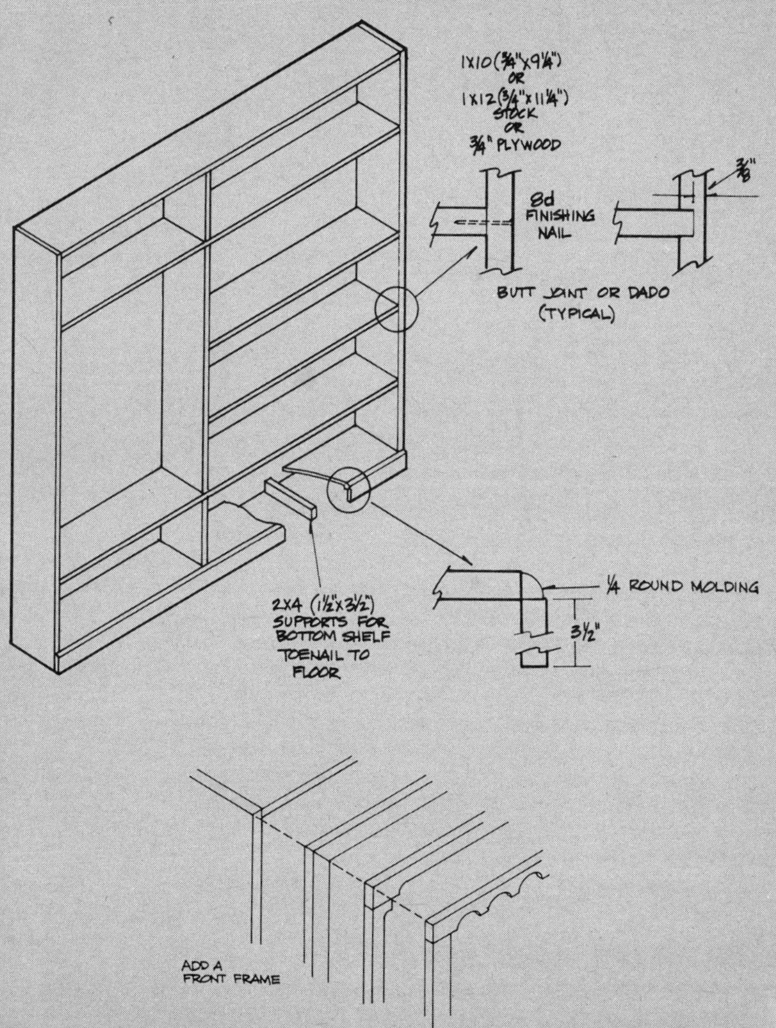
1X10 (3/4"X9 1/4")
OR
1X12 (3/4"X11 1/4")
STOCK
OR
3/4" PLYWOOD
8d
FINISHING
NAIL
3/8"
BUTT JOINT OR DADO
(TYPICAL)
1/4 ROUND MOLDING
3 1/2"
2X4 (1 1/2"X3 1/2")
SUPPORTS FOR
BOTTOM SHELF
TOENAIL TO
FLOOR
ADD A
FRONT FRAME

## A VERY BASIC DISPLAY SHELF

1 1 x 1 shelf cleat — nail into each stud with 10d finishing nails.
2 Shelf (¾″ stock) — nail into cleat (between studs) with 4d finishing nails.
3 Brackets — shape with coping saw or saber saw — nail into stud as shown — nail through shelf into brackets with 6d finishing nails.

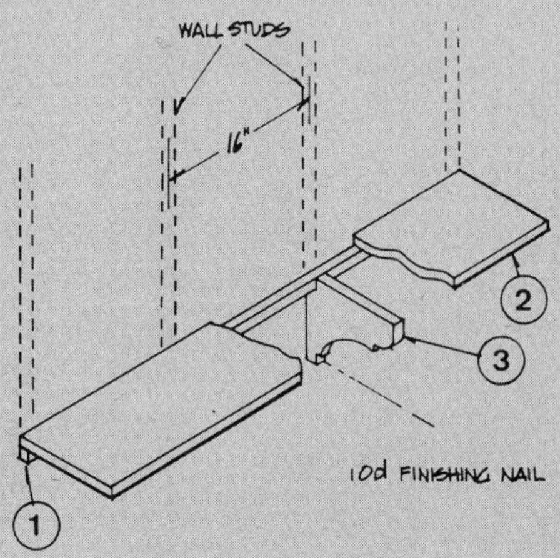


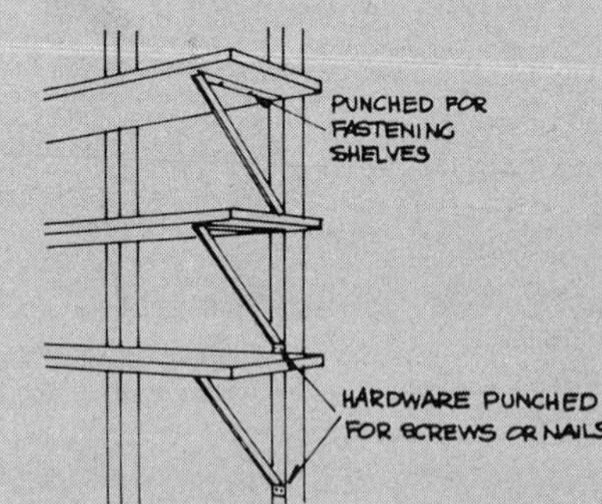


Ready-to-use shelf hardware doesn't have to be fancy. Hardware for utility shelves like those you might want to mount against the open studs in a garage is available. Secure the brackets, place the shelf boards — instant storage capacity!

# 3/ GREAT HOME IMPROVEMENT POSSIBILITIES

As we were preparing this book, we realized that plans for the larger projects would demand too much space for a book this size . . . and we'd rather use that space to show you more easily adaptable home improvement ideas. We are therefore offering you the opportunity to purchase a complete set of plans at the nominal cost of $2.50 for each plan. The key to success with these larger projects is firm attention to detail. Follow instructions carefully, and the elegance these plans provide can be yours. Analyze the project ideas thoroughly so that you choose the best variation offered in any project. Take a good, long look at the rest of your home to ensure that the style of the addition you've chosen will blend happily with what's already there. Each plan has a number. You can order from the form on page 207.

6
4
5
3
2
1

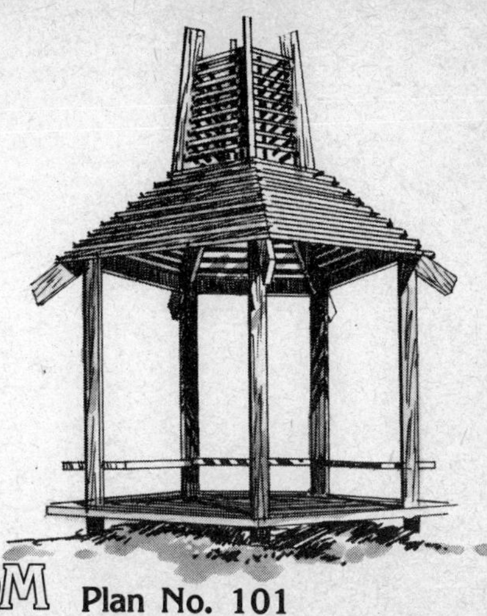

# THE GAZEBO— A GAZING ROOM

## Plan No. 101

"Gazebo" comes from the Latin *videbo,* probably not etymologically correct, but it conveys the idea. A gazebo is a quiet place for gazing, where muscle and mind unwind. The mood is catching. Words are softly spoken, drinks are sipped. What a charming retreat in this fast-paced world — a therapy room you can build yourself.

The gazebo is a freestanding structure, sometimes with a touch of wall (like wainscoting) or an attractive railing, sometimes with full walls on two or three sides built with fancy latticework, but always sturdy and light and airy. Once the basic gazebo is done, additions come easily. The plans cover all the essentials, show ideas, make suggestions.

Some points covered include:

1. The base. It can be simple, like small concrete pads supporting concrete blocks which in turn hold beams for the floor. Or you can pour a concrete slab or erect a small deck.
2. The floor. Wood or concrete, brick or tile? You may have an in-place floor you can build on.
3. Structural supports. They must do the job and look good. A type of post-and-beam design makes sense because it has the necessary strength and few components to obstruct the view.
4. The cover. Closed or open — we show you how to frame for it and the materials to use.
5. Decorative touches. They're optional, but you may wish to add them sooner or later.
6. A cupola. Add it for appearance or for increased ventilation if you cover the gazebo with a solid roof.

# SUNSHADES Plan No. 102

Sunshades are often called "trellises" since they can be light and airy and frequently are used as espaliers for vines. Essentially, they are overhead constructions whose purpose is to filter the sun's rays, creating a pleasant, open atmosphere that contributes much to outdoor relaxation. The use of a deciduous vine as a cover, while not critical, makes sense since the plant affords maximum protection during summer months, but, having dropped its leaves, allows more of the sun to come through when the weather turns cold.

A sunshade can project from a house wall and be situated over an existing patio or deck, or it can be a freestanding unit, isolated a bit so it serves as a private retreat. Where and how it is placed affects how it should be erected.

5
4
2
1

Light and airy is fine, but that doesn't mean it should be fragile. Our plans tell you how to achieve attractive, durable results.

A few essentials:

1. The floor. We show how to organize the project if the sunshade will cover an existing patio or deck. Available pieces of hardware make post attachments quite simple. There are a number of ways to go if the project is freestanding.

2. The main supports. We cover materials, sizes, spacing.

3. Joists. What you use affects appearance, i.e., solid beams, doubled 2" material, methods of securing to posts.

4. The structure that projects from the house wall. How do you secure the joists? Maybe lock them to roof rafters with bolts. Setting up a ledger that is spiked to wall studs is another way.

5. The cover. How much filtration will you want? Your decision affects what you should see — 2x4s, lath strips, maybe rain-proofing with sheets of fiberglass.

6. Sidewalls. These are not always included, but may be needed as a windbreak or for privacy; but they must not be solid. The wall must do its job without blocking light and air.

4
3
6
2

# Plan No. 103 DECKS—NATURAL OUTDOOR FLOORS

Decks are for lounging and reading, for daydreaming or sun-bathing, for family groups, parties, outdoor dining. Few structures are as compatible with trees, grass, flowers, and shrubs as a wood deck, and few projects can immediately add so much to your lifestyle and the value of your home.

A deck should be a personal thing, and it must suit a particular environment. Yet decks are structurally similar so that a homeowner, armed with ideas and essential construction details, will not find construction a formidable task.

Our deck plans anticipate questions and possible problems:

1. Deck foundations. On precast concrete piers spanned with beams, sturdy pressure-treated posts are set in the ground. A grade-level deck can rest on a thick bed of tamped gravel.

2. Flooring. Tongue-and-groove boards, 2x4s placed flat, or square-edge boards can be spaced for drainage. Consider 1⅛" thick exterior grade plywood underlayment topped with indoor/outdoor carpeting.

3. Railings. Attached to floor supports, extensions of posts are set up on a plate nailed to the floor.

4. Multi-level deck. How do you step up or down safely? The general rule is: the wider the tread, the shorter the riser.

5. Fascia strips. They are seldom included, but are a nice touch that ends the project professionally.

6. A built-in bench. Plan for it at the beginning so it's an integral component. Exclusive touches like this set your handiwork apart.

5
4
2
3
1

# FENCES—TO SURROUND YOU NATURALLY

## Plan No. 104

Too often fences are viewed as necessary barriers and designed to demand "keep out!" instead of asking "please don't." A fence doesn't have to be dictatorial. Actually, it doesn't even have to be a "fence." It can be a screen, a windbreak, or a sunshade, a way to hide a utility area, a patio divider, a backdrop for shrubs, an espalier for vines — options infinite! The solid, vertical-board fence has its place, but isn't the only way to go, as our plans reveal. Often, the difference between prosaic and creative is determined by how materials are used, not how much they cost.

All fences, regardless of design, have common structural aspects. Strength is a most important factor since such structures are usually free-standing. Posts, rails, and cover materials must work together for the project to be long-lived. Some of the materials covered in the plans:

1. Setting posts. The correct way to form post holes (you don't use a shovel). Concrete encasement and a subbase of gravel for drainage.

2. Post size and texture. A smooth or a rough finish — both are available so you can make a choice in relation to the effect you want.

3. Rail-to-post joints. Toenailed butt joint, a dado, blocking, a notch? Much depends on the tools you have to work with and the effort you're willing to contribute.

4. Cover materials. You can choose vertical boards, a lattice effect, boards placed horizontally or diagonally. Exterior plywood siding is a super material for fence projects and available in many patterns and textures.

5. Some exclusive touches. A top rail placed away from the solid portion provides additional fence height without making the project more forbidding.

1
5
4
3
2
6

Plan No. 105

# ALL-PURPOSE OUTDOOR SHED

When following our plans for this unique concept in outdoor sheds, you'll be creating for yourself a most useful structure. Although our construction information is specific, there are options that allow customizing the project exactly to your needs. It can be used as storage for garden tools, furniture, other equipment; or add a bench — maybe a window — and you have a potting shed with ample storage space for related materials.

Size options allow you to build one unit or two. Units can face each other with a walk-through aisle between them, or you can add a common roof and close it in for a tight little building.

Some of the points the plans cover:

1. Overall size. Plans utilize standard-size materials so there will be a minimum of cutting and waste.

2. Base for the shed. A base must be easy to clean and walk on. Will a concrete slab do? You may want a deck larger than the building so you can set up a lounge and a barbecue.

3. The framing. Standard studs — but placed 24″ on centers — will do and will cut down on costs. The spacing will still accommodate standard-width plywood sidings.

4. Siding. Choices are almost infinite: smooth surfaces, textures, grooves; fir, cedar, redwood, pine. There is a special plywood (MDO — Medium Density Overlaid) that is easily painted.

5. Roof cover. Shakes, shingles, mineral-surfaced saturated felt are all easy to apply, durable, and economical. What appeals to you?

6. Closing in. In framing for a door, door width is important. 36″ is the minimum.

4
5
2
3
6
1

# Plan No. 106 GABLE GREENHOUSE

The first person to envision a greenhouse didn't know it, but he anticipated the solar home, for that's what a greenhouse is — for plants, not people. A greenhouse utilizes the sun's heat passively and can be therapeutic, or simply practical, or both. Grow and show exotic plants; use as a bedding place for seedlings; develop a year-round source of vegetables. It is a worthwhile project with substantial returns and is within the scope of any craftsperson with the plans we make available.

The gable concept is straightforward and has high sidewalls for tall plants, plenty of headroom. Construction procedures involve simple cuts you can accomplish with a handsaw.

The plans include descriptions of the following:

1. The floor. It can be soil, tamped and moisture-free, or a concrete slab for easier-to-clean, surer footing.
2. The framework. A conventional approach is easiest to do and most economical. We'll tell you what to do if the floor is soil, what to do if it is a concrete slab.
3. Covers. They function like windows to let the light in; they enclose to retain heat; they fight the intrusion of snow, wind, or rain; and they say "no" to animals and insects. There are several ways to go — glass, rigid plastic, sheet plastic. Glass is an old and traditional cover material. Rigid plastic is a reasonable substitute. Film plastic is easy to apply, but will probably have to be replaced on a regular schedule.
4. Ventilation. Adjustable vents make sense. They help to control interior temperatures.
5. The entry door. A readymade door won't do, but the plans will tell how to frame for one that can be covered with the same material used on the house.
6. The interior. Shelves make it easy to utilize a maximum amount of space. The plans show how to attach shelves directly to framing members.

before
1
6
3
2
5
4
after

# A BAY WINDOW— A GARDEN WINDOW Plan No. 107

Structurally, this project allows you a choice. Use the extra space for a seat, which is a true bay window, or for a garden. In the latter case the existing floor is extended, and since the exterior is mostly glass, there is light for the plants and for the room as a whole.

Perimeter walls are *bearing* walls, that is, they provide support for what is above and for that reason demand special consideration. If the new project utilizes an existing window, then structural considerations are minimized; the in-place header will do its job despite the remodeling. If you choose a wider opening, you'll need a longer header.

The following are some of the essential factors covered in the plans:

1. The header. If a new one is needed, a 4x12 beam (common in modern constructions) will solve all problems, but it must be installed just so.
2. Exterior components. They must relate to a bay window or a garden window.
3. Garden window. All connections must be waterproof. We'll tell you what materials and what joints you'll need.
4. The floor extension. It won't be needed if you construct a bay window, but a garden window requires one. How do you extend the existing floor? Will you pour an additional concrete slab or extend the house floor joists?
5. A window seat. It's done like a knee wall with a top-side cover for whatever you use as a pad. Standard materials are used — 2x4s, plywood, prefinished paneling or gypsum board to finish inside surfaces.
6. Glass for the garden window. You'll need to know what kind you want and how it should be installed. Waterproofing is essential.

# A PLACE CALLED TETE-A-TETE Plan No. 108

A "tete-a-tete" is a special seat, S-shaped so two can sit face-to-face. The modern version, for groups instead of twosomes, is called a conversation pit, probably because in new constructions the site for the seats is provided by a step-down area in the room. Our idea adopts the concept, but is not so restrictive. Our detailed plans lead you through the construction phases, but placement is flexible. Grouped with a cocktail table, arranged for coziness with a fireplace — place the units on the finished floor or set them before you lay carpeting for a built-in look. The projects are handsome enough for use anywhere, placed as you would conventional pieces.

The plans are detailed and include:

1. Overall. How high, how long, how wide — all very important since comfort is as important as appearance.
2. The framework. It must combine construction simplicity with strength. 2x4s can be used, but they must be dry. No twisting allowed after the skeleton is covered.
3. Cover materials. There are many options, especially if you choose from the host of decorative wall panelings that are available. You may want to consider using the same material that is now on the walls of the room.
4. Pad or cushion supports. Plywood will do since the projects are designed for use with thick foam rubber pads covered with a material of your choice. It's also possible to work with large readymade cushions.
5. A wide ledge — tile covered? You can apply an exotic tile directly to wood with a mastic. It's like having an attached perimeter table with a soil-proof surface. A wet glass can't hurt it.

1
2
3
4
5

# LIBATION CENTER Plan No. 109

It's fun to play at bartending, but only when all is organized so the job can be done efficiently. Our plans are for a unit a professional wouldn't mind using, and it can be established almost anywhere — in the family room, playroom, remodeled basement, wherever gatherings make the home bar desirable.

Of course the bar can't stand only on appearance; it must be efficient. Adequate storage space, correct height, maintenance-free and waterproof surfaces, a front cap for the counter, a bar rail (not critical but nice) — these are all things to think about and include.

Some of the thoughts that are covered in our plans:

1. Overall. A bar is not a counter or a table. Its height should relate to the standard height of bar stools. Whether the bar is straight or L-shaped, the space behind it should permit bartender freedom. The structure is a skeleton frame of standard materials, designed for shelves and easily covered with prefinished paneling.
2. The surface. How wide? It should be easy to clean and waterproof. One option is thick, exterior grade plywood veneered with a plastic laminate.
3. A front cap. This is standard on bars, but it can be difficult and expensive to imitate. Our plans suggest an easy way — readily available window "stool," a standard moulding that requires a modifying cut that the plans will describe.

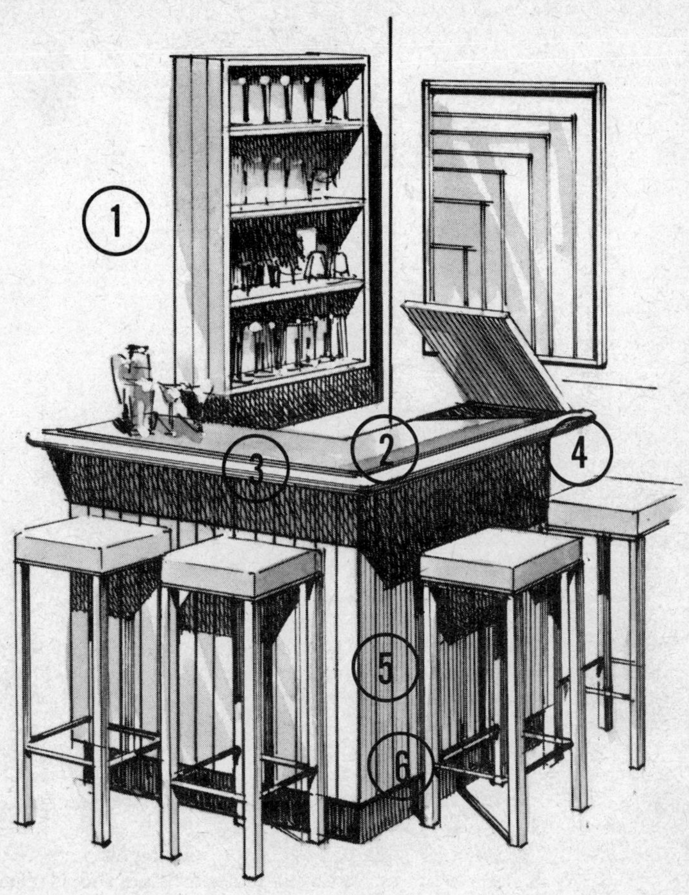


4. Counter "overhang." The bar is most comfortable when the thickness of the counter is minimized and the overhang is enough so "patrons" can snuggle up.

5. Covers. The easiest and most attractive material is wall paneling in a choice of textures and wood species. It's prefinished, so attach it and forget it.

6. The bar rail. Remember the "brass rail?" You don't have to go that way, but a foot rest is accommodating and nostalgic. The plans suggest aluminum tubing, heavy wood dowel — maybe just a narrow wood shelf.

# TWO BEDS FOR THE SPACE OF ONE Plan No. 110

Bunk beds can make a small room larger or turn a large room into a combination bedroom/playroom. They're ideal for children of similar age (though chances are they'll skirmish for the top one); but even if used in a one-child room, they are practical since they provide for the little one's overnight guests.

Bunk beds can be adventurous, but a nuisance if they are not designed with the maintainer as well as the user in mind. Our plans consider these factors and others. For example, the lower bunk will be most convenient if made as a slip-in unit, mounted on readily available casters so it can be pulled away from the wall for easy bed-making and for an occasional change in position.

Other factors the plans consider:

1. Materials. A good-looking hardwood plywood can be the basic material, but what thickness, and how do you conceal edges?
2. Top bunk height. It can't be arbitrary. The top bed has to be made, and the average person is not eight feet tall.
3. Mattress supports. Plywood will work, but slats might be better since they permit air to circulate. How to attach and support them? It's important for safety. Mattress size? Why not a standard one (30″ x 75″), easy to buy anywhere.
4. Lower bunk. It can be built in, but as we said, it will be more convenient to make up if it can roll out.
5. Ladder. Of course it must be sturdy, but how should you make it? Heavy dowel, aluminum tubing, maybe just flat ladder rungs — these are the choices.
6. Finishing touches. Provide shelves for books, a radio, a light. These are added details that make the project a happier place. You may not have to fight to get the kids to bed.

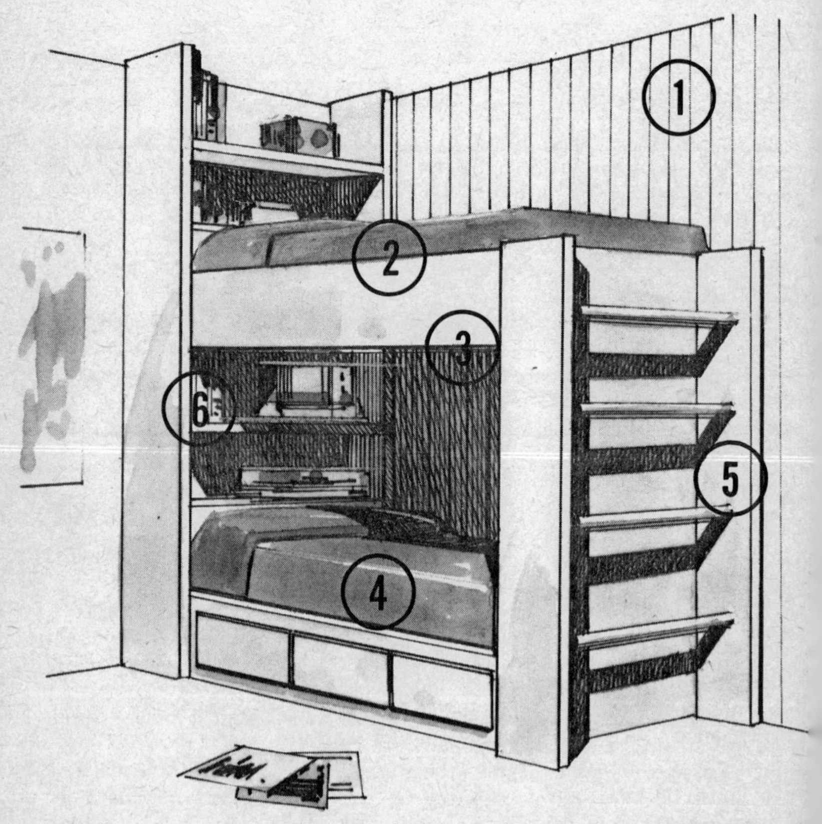
1
2
3
4
5
6

# 4/ HOW TO CREATE DECORATIVE ELEGANCE

There are many possibilities for "fixed" projects throughout the home that are really fairly simple to accomplish, yet they give the home that little extra "finished" look. Take paneling, for instance. There are many ways to use paneling materials beyond the standard application. There are numerous effects you can create with paneling if you plan well. In this section of the book we offer a variety of ideas with paneling and other materials, as well as some diagrammatic details to help you over the rough spots when you get ready to do your project. It is very important to ascertain in advance that your project will complement your existing environment. Also, pay attention to all of the details, because when you're attempting to enhance your home's appeal, any flaws in your project performance will be around for some time to come.

# A NEW ENTRY— A NEW APPROACH

The single-door entry, often with an approach that's only a few concrete steps and a small landing or a minimum concrete pad, is drab and uninviting. It establishes a mood that doesn't reveal the dedicated homeowner's care and pride. Startling psychological changes accompany the physical ones when you remodel to a double door — or add a glass panel — and follow with an attractive entry deck. Suddenly everything is wide and handsome and more hospitable.

Outside house walls are bearing walls, so changing to a double door means you must replace the existing header with one that will span the new opening. Mark the outline of the opening on the outside of the house and remove as little of the siding as necessary. If the siding is plywood, remove full panels. If the siding is horizontal boards, make a cut on the line you have established. Your best bet is to use a circular saw with blade projection set to match the thickness of the siding. With the siding removed, you can check the void in the wall for anything that might have to be re-routed — for example, electric wires leading to an entry light.

One of the studs you must remove can be relocated as the outline stud for the new header. The trimmer you removed when you broke down the old door frame can also be reused. What you have done is duplicate the original framing, but with a longer header.

Work carefully when you replace old siding or add new pieces. Finishing is done in a conventional manner — jambs and stops for the doors, a new sill, and, finally, new trim material both inside and out.

The procedure for adding a glass pane is similar except that you don't remove the existing door header. You do add a new header, an outline stud, and two new trimmers. The detail drawing shows how to trim for the new glass panel.

## A NEW ENTRY (cont'd)

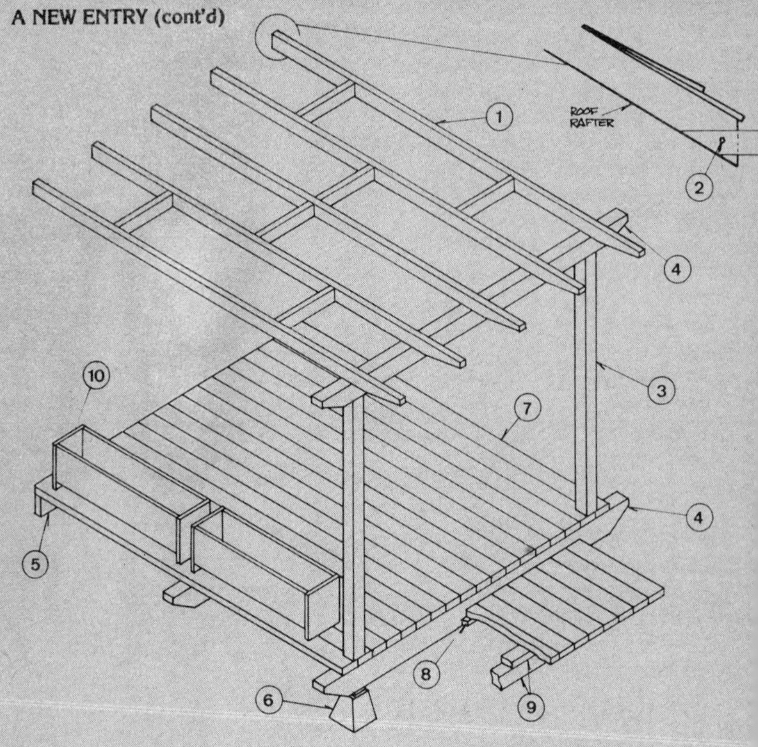


NEW APPROACH FOR THE NEW ENTRY

1 2x4s
2 ⅜″ x 4″ carriage bolts
3 4x4s
4 4x6 or 4x8 beams
5 2x6 ledger secured to house wall
6 precast concrete pier (on poured footing)
7 2x6 tongue and groove boards or spaced, square-edge boards
8 2x ledger
9 poured concrete ribbon with attached 2x treated nailer
10 planters

## THE NEW APPROACH

The drawing shows a design that applies when the entry is a foot or more above grade. Floor support beams rest on precast concrete piers that are set on poured concrete pads. The piers do not have to be totally above grade; it depends on how much height (distance from grade to door sill) you have to work with. The idea is to eliminate soil-wood contact areas. The concrete ribbon suggested as a support for the outboard end of the step boards does not have to be very large; 8″ deep x 4″ wide is more than enough. The nailer can be attached with anchor bolts just as you would secure the sill plate in a house frame.

There are a couple of ways to go when the entry deck can't be elevated. If there is a slab and a step-up into the house, deck-board supports can be pressure-treated lumber (as small as 2x4s) placed directly on the slab and secured with case-hardened nails or with bolts threaded into expansion sleeves that have been set in holes drilled in the concrete.

There is a solution if the deck must be at grade level. Excavate the deck area to a depth of about 8″. Dampen and tamp the base so it is as solid as you can make it. Fill the excavation to a depth of about 4″ with gravel. Tamp the gravel and level it. The gravel provides a base for pressure-treated 4x4s to which you nail the deck boards. Projects like this call for attention to good drainage. A slight slope to a run-off area is one solution. Another is a shallow perimeter trough to collect water and direct it away from the house.

Above-deck constructions apply regardless of how the floor is placed — 4x4 posts spanned with beams that support rafters projecting from the house wall. The deck rafters are locked to house rafters with carriage bolts and to the beam by toenailing.

Our design shows a trellis-like cover for the deck. This is suitable as is or as a support for a flowering vine. If you wish to rain-proof it, you can add panels of corrugated fiberglass which provide protection without eliminating light.

## MATERIALS

Cedar, redwood, or cypress are natural candidates because they are handsome woods with built-in resistance to damage caused by rot, decay, and insects; but pine, fir, larch, hemlock, and others can be used and might be more compatible with existing decor. The point is that most species will do if treated with preservatives or if other means are taken — like coatings of paint — to extend useful life.

In soil-contact or even near soil-contact situations, use wood that is naturally resistant or pressure treated or which you treat with a preservative. In other areas, where only moisture can be a villain, wood can be treated with exterior type sealers, siding stains, or paint.

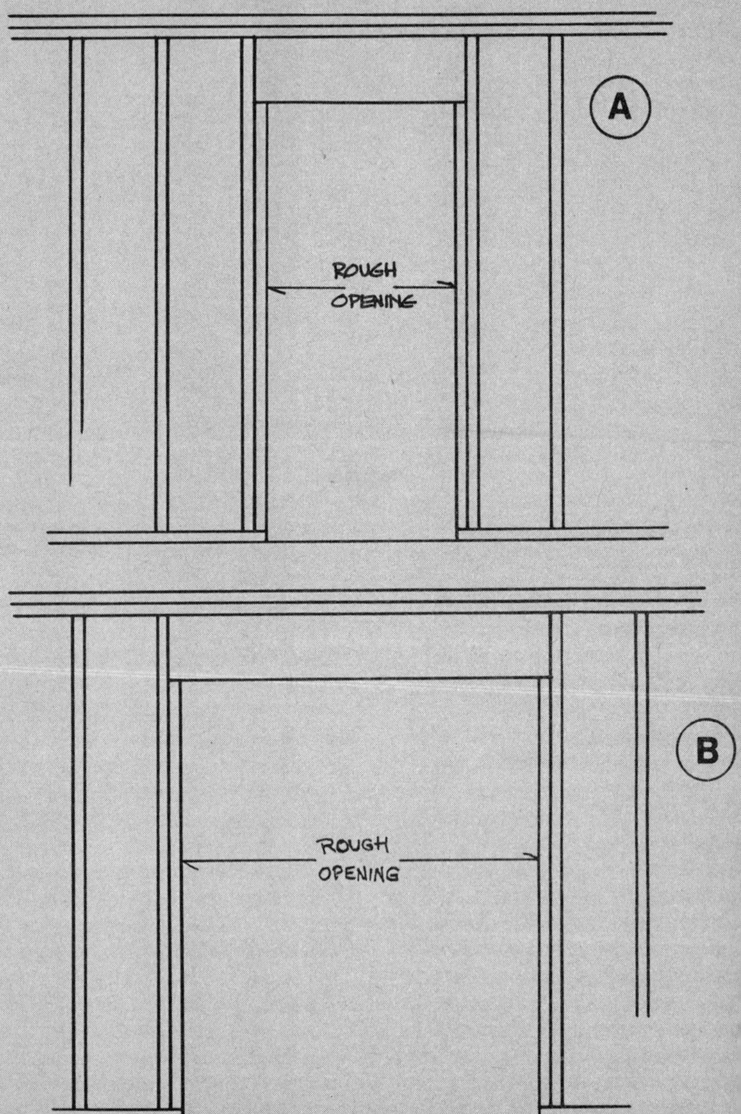
A
ROUGH OPENING
B
ROUGH OPENING

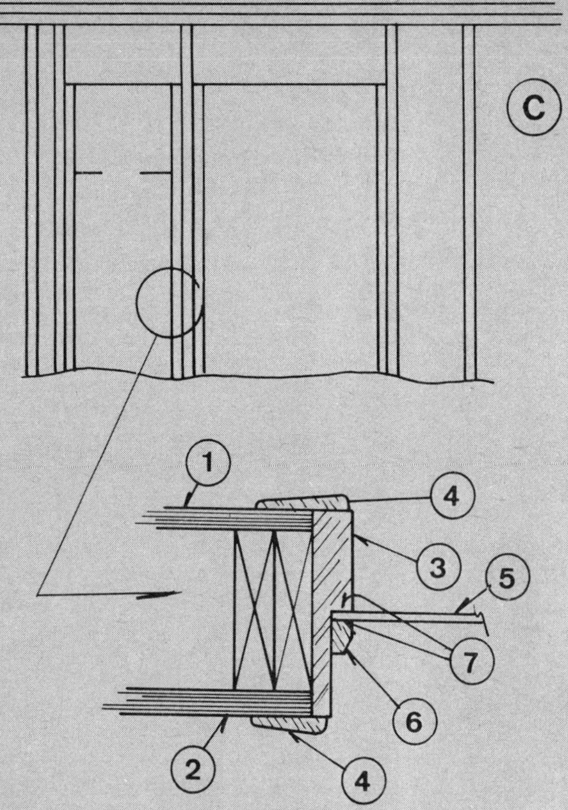


A NEW ENTRY

A Framing for an existing single door — the rough opening will be the width of the door (36″) plus thickness of the jambs (usually 2(¾″)) plus leeway between jambs and trimmers so jambs can be set plumb (usually between ¾″ and 1″).

B To install double doors — erect new header — rough opening increases by width of second door.

C Increase inside light by adding a glass pane — install new header — rough opening equals width of glass.

1 inside wall cover
2 siding
3 rabbeted jamb stock
4 trim
5 glass
6 stop
7 caulking

# THE HOW-TO OF WALL PANELING

Few wall coverings are as effective or as easy to apply as decorative wall panelings, and the appearance choices are broad enough for any situation. Choose from contemporary, rustic, or an old world feeling. Decide after checking panels displayed by a local supplier; or make the decision first and then see what's available. Chances are excellent you'll find something exactly right.

Here's more enticement: the panels are large, 4′ x 8′, yet light enough for one-person handling. Place one and you immediately have 32 square feet of new, easily maintained wall. It's an attractive and practical way to go.

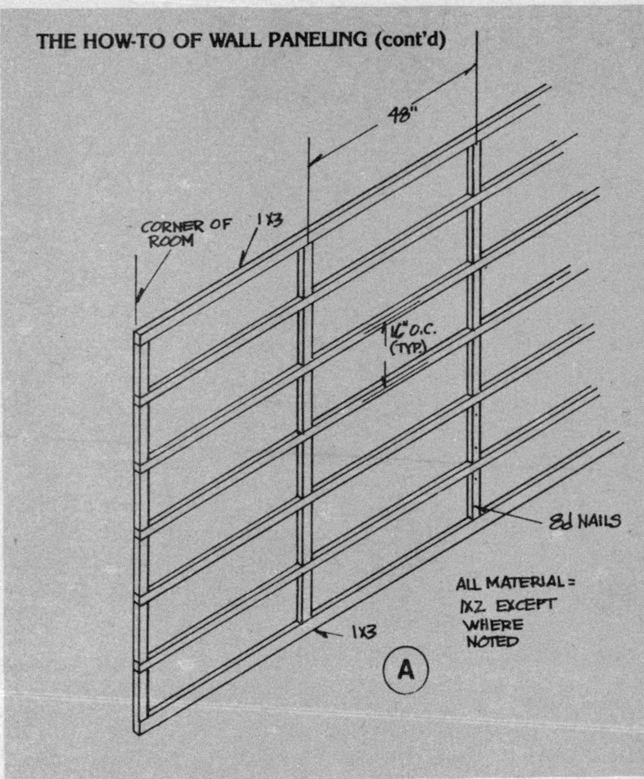


## HOW MANY PANELS?

The room's perimeter will tell you. Assume a room measures 15′ x 18′. Two (15′) plus two (18′) equals 66′. Panels are 4′ wide, so 66′ divided by 4′ comes out as 16½ panels. Door, window, fireplace areas are deductible: about half a panel for each usually works out; but, of course, these are variables, so measuring for the deductions is wise. You don't buy half panels. If your arithmetic says 14½ panels, buy 15. Be generous — it's better than being short. Extra paneling can be useful — for matching cornice or a shield for concealed lighting. Many people use the same paneling as a veneer on existing doors.

## APPLICATION

If walls are sound and true, paneling may be applied directly with nails o

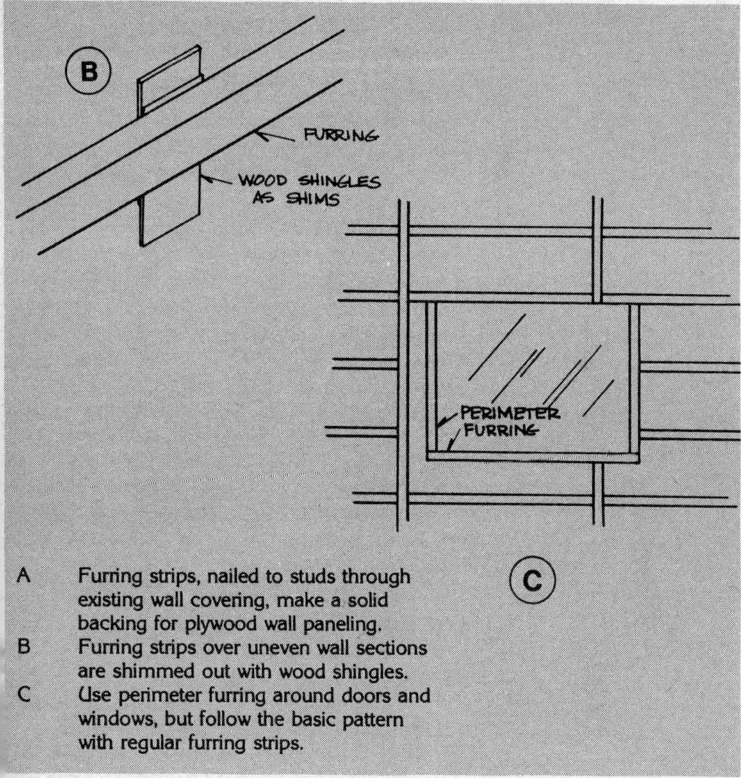


A Furring strips, nailed to studs through existing wall covering, make a solid backing for plywood wall paneling.
B Furring strips over uneven wall sections are shimmed out with wood shingles.
C Use perimeter furring around doors and windows, but follow the basic pattern with regular furring strips.

glue. Most times when remodeling, it's been found that covering the wall with a gridwork of furring strips solves all problems. Usually 1 x 2 sound, dry lumber is used, but plywood is a good candidate. Plywood furring can be as thin as ⅜", as wide as 2". "Scrap" pieces of ¾" plywood ripped into 2" strips make excellent furring.

In any event, the furring is applied as shown in the drawing — verticals, 48" on centers (over studs); horizontals, 16" on centers and nailed at each stud crossing. The horizontal pieces will be easy to install if you make a special gauge — a piece of wood that is 16" long, less the width of one furring piece. Thus, if furring is 1½" wide, the spacing gauge will be 14½" long.

The joint between horizontal and vertical strips must not be tight. Also, leave a gap of about ¼" between the top strip and the ceiling and between the bottom strip and the floor to allow for breather space.

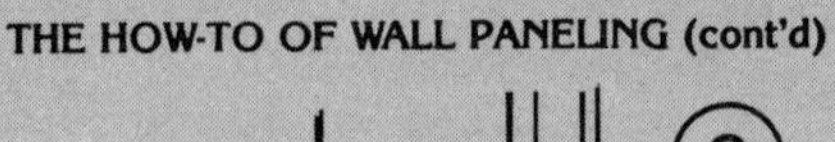

## THE HOW-TO OF WALL PANELING (cont'd)

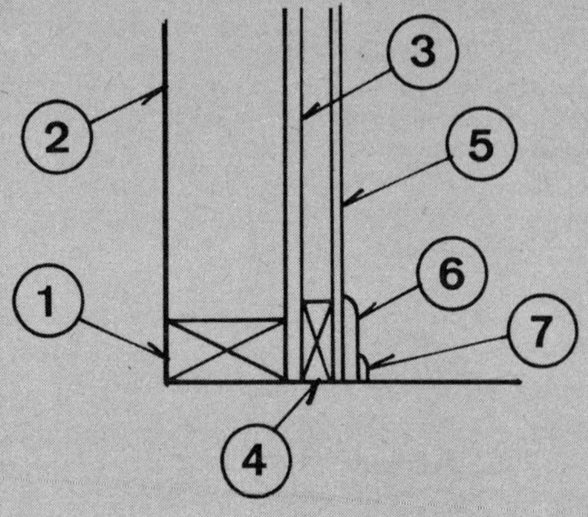


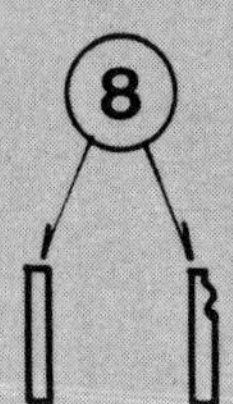


FINISHING AT THE FLOOR LINE

1 sole plate
2 studs
3 existing wall covering
4 furring
5 new paneling
6 baseboards
7 shoe (optional)
8 baseboard may be plain board or it can be fancy

### POSITIONING THE PANELS

First, spread the panels around the room so you can judge the best placement in relation to tone and grain pattern. Number the panels on the back so you'll know where each will go.

The first panel goes in a corner, placed so its free edge hits the center of a vertical furring strip. Use a level to be sure the panel is perfectly vertical. You may have to reshape the corner edge of the panel if the room corner is not plumb. If the panel abuts an irregular wall — a brick or a stone surface — you'll have to shape the panel's edge accordingly. Best way is to hold the panel in place and then work with a compass, using the irregular wall as a guide so you can transfer the cut-line to the panel. If the cut-line is straight, saw with a crosscut saw. If irregular, use a coping saw or saber saw. With a coping saw or

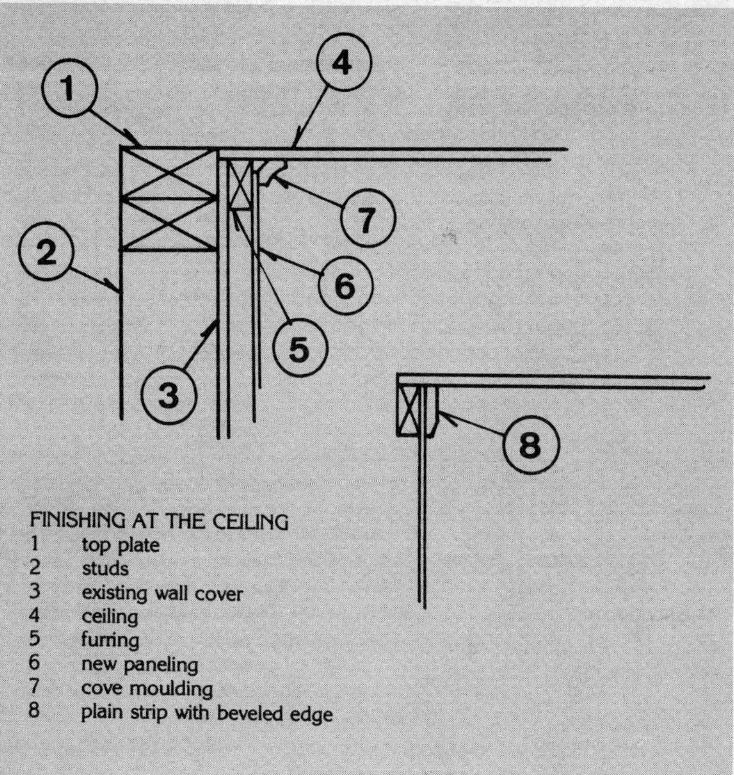


FINISHING AT THE CEILING
1 top plate
2 studs
3 existing wall cover
4 ceiling
5 furring
6 new paneling
7 cove moulding
8 plain strip with beveled edge

crosscut saw, keep the good side of the panel up. Do the reverse with a saber saw.

Once the first panel is up, others will install rather quickly. Simply butt edges, glue, and nail in place. Use 3d finishing nails, spacing them 8″ along all edges and 16″ along horizontal furring. Set nail heads about 1/32″ deep, then conceal them with a putty stick. The colored sticks are available to match the tone of the paneling.

The detail drawings show how to finish professionally in corners, around doors and windows, and at floor and ceiling joints. Matching mouldings for the paneling you have installed are available. Unfinished mouldings in a wide variety are also available should you decide to do your own thing.

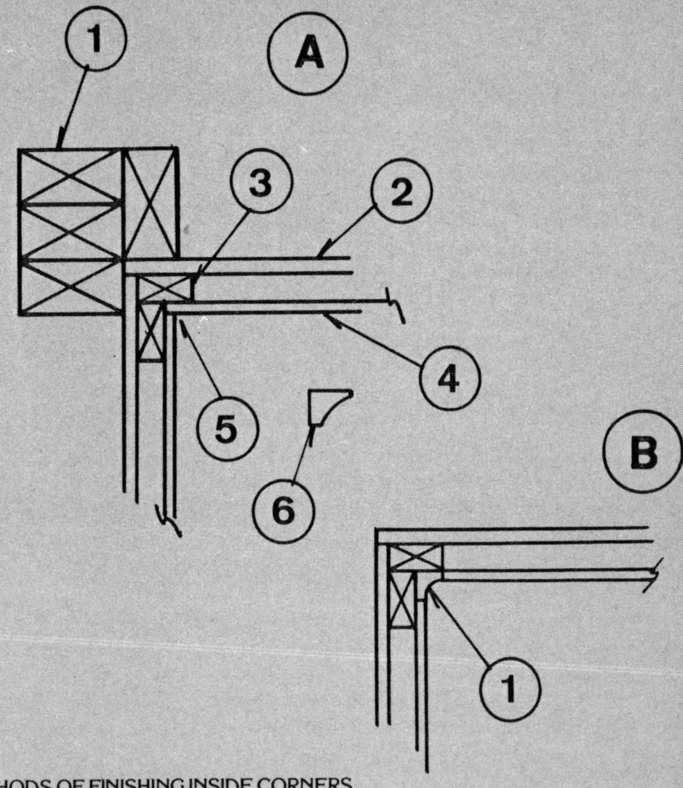


METHODS OF FINISHING INSIDE CORNERS

A 1 typical corner post framing
2 existing wall covering
3 furring (necessary for uneven or untrue walls)
4 new plywood paneling
5 simple butt joint
6 Butt joint may be covered with moulding.

B 1 Paneling may be butted against moulding.

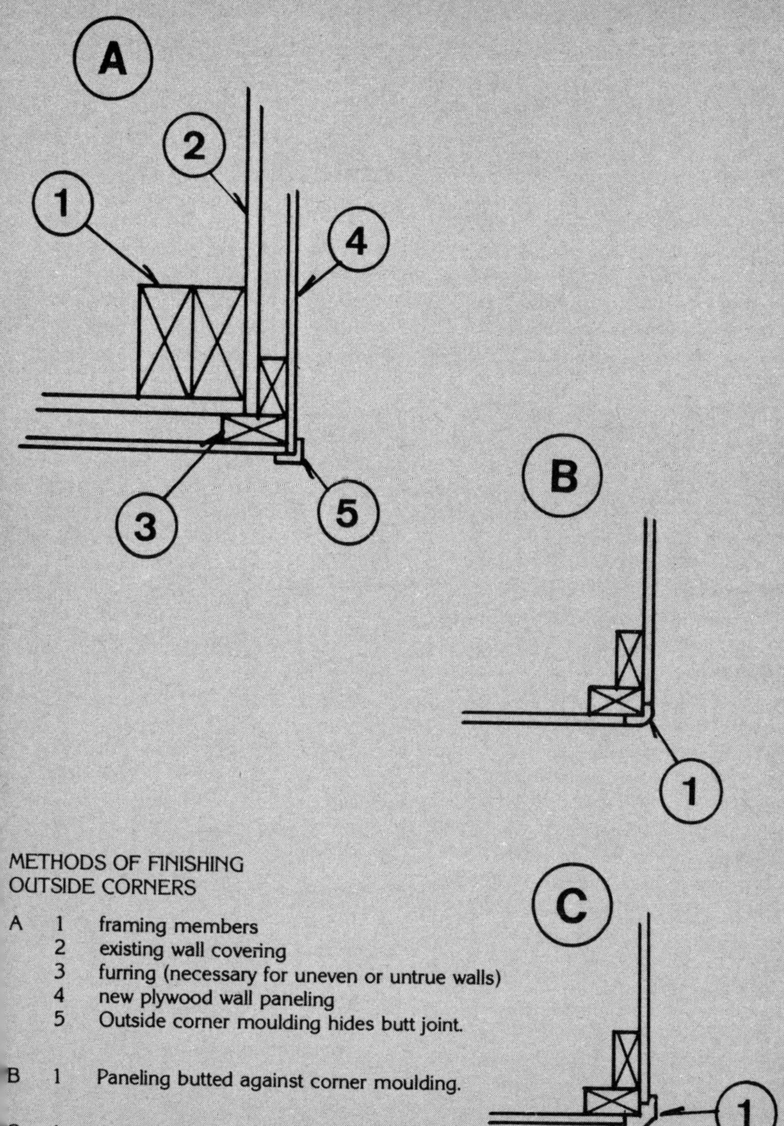


METHODS OF FINISHING
OUTSIDE CORNERS

A 1 framing members
2 existing wall covering
3 furring (necessary for uneven or untrue walls)
4 new plywood wall paneling
5 Outside corner moulding hides butt joint.

B 1 Paneling butted against corner moulding.

C 1 custom-made moulding

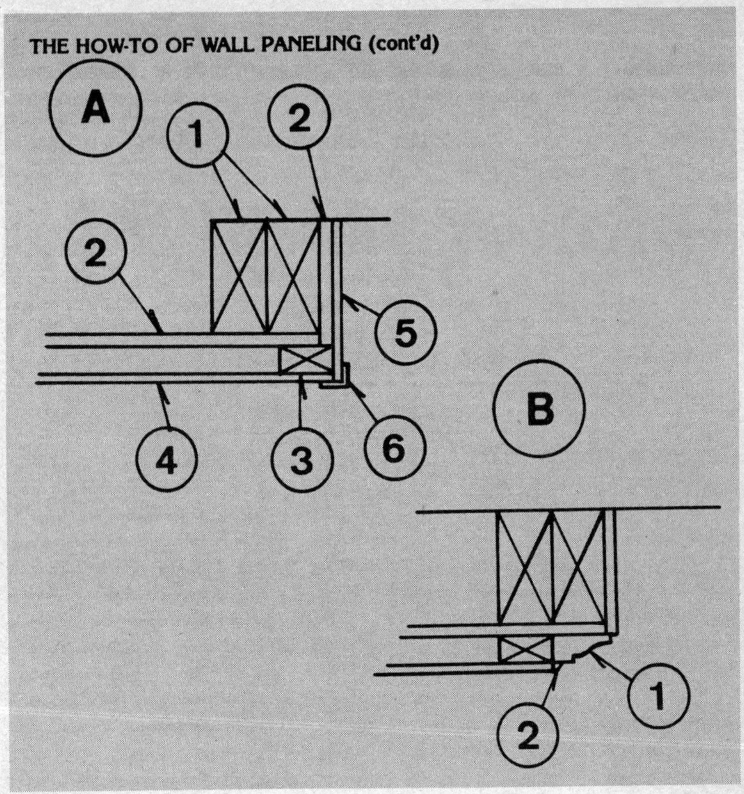


## POINTS TO CONSIDER

Existing mouldings, if carefully removed, may be reusable. Existing baseboard, if of correct thickness and not saved for reuse, can serve as the bottom furring strip. All edges of each panel must be attached to furring. Add extra strips if necessary. Use a block plane or something similar to slightly bevel the back edges of panels that abut. Leave a ¼″ gap at top, bottom, and ends of installations so panels can expand if necessary. Mouldings hide the gaps. It's a good idea to store the panels in the room for a few days before installation. This is to allow moisture content to equalize.

Application of paneling is not difficult, but accurate measuring and careful sawing and fitting are the keys to a successful project. This is one situation where it pays to use an hour to do a half-hour job. The paneling will be nice to look at for a long time.

METHODS OF FINISHING AROUND DOORS AND WINDOWS

A
1. stud and trimmer
2. existing wall cover
3. furring (necessary for uneven or untrue walls)
4. new paneling
5. paneling carried around corner
6. outside corner moulding

B
1. new or salvaged trim
2. ¼ round moulding

Note that perimeter furring is set back.

C
1. custom-made moulding/trim

D
New jamb may be installed in doorway.
1. New jamb is wider by combined thickness of furring and paneling.
2. conventional casing

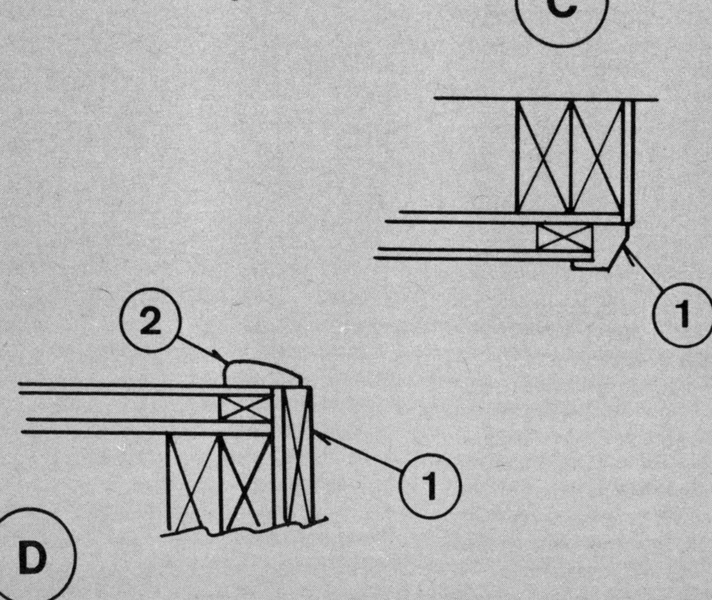

# HOW TO ADD CEILING BEAMS

These are pseudo beams in the sense that they are not structural members. They do not provide support for the ceiling; joists, spanning across the top wall plates, do that. Ours are added for the feeling of solidity and the decorative detail they provide. They can be rugged like some of yesterday's true house members — or they can be sleek to fit any modern decor. They can be hollow — a U-shaped structure — or they can be solid 2x4s or 2x6s, either finished or in the rough. If finished they will actually measure 1½" x 3¼" or 1½" x 5½". If in the rough, they will measure what you ask for, maybe even a bit more. The finished pieces will be smooth, the rough pieces will have a deeper textured appearance that may fit general decor. An advantage of the built-up beam — the U-shaped structure — is that you can decide its width and depth, and it's a passageway for electrical wiring, even a plumbing pipe.

Attach solid pieces with lag screws driven into joists. These, if painted flat black, can be left exposed — a treatment especially suitable in a room that has

before

after

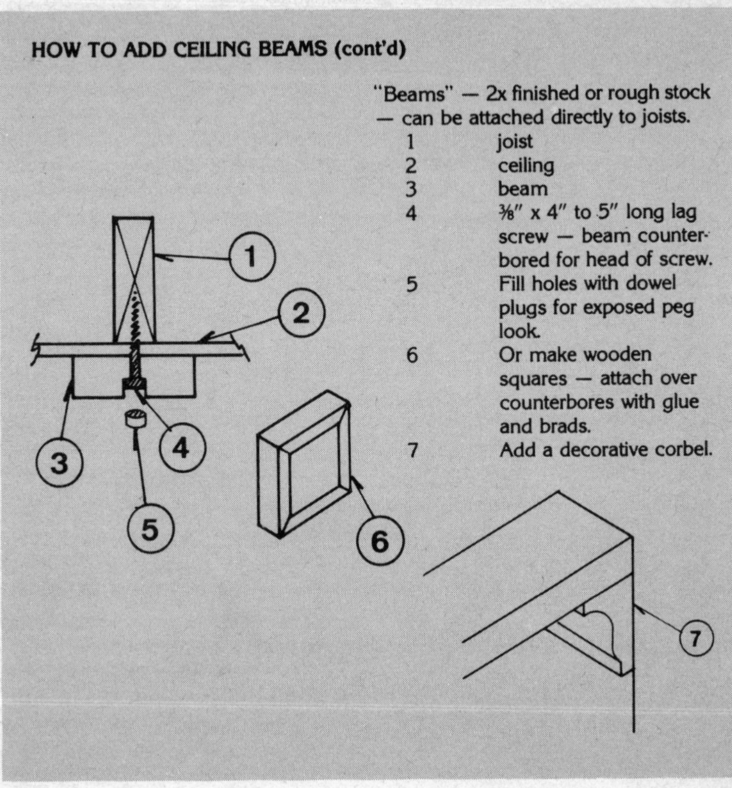


wrought iron accents. To hide them, form a counterbore for the screw's head so it can be covered with a dowel plug or a specially made small square of wood. If you lack a counterbore, do the job this way. Use a spade bit to form the seat for the screw's shank. In any event, since the screws or their covers will be exposed, space the screws nicely across the length of the beam.

For hollow beams, the nailers (beam supports) can be secured to joists with nails. Use box or common nails that are as long as the combined thickness of ceiling and nailer plus about 2½". As the drawings show, there are many ways to build up the beams: plain boards, mouldings, plain boards plus mouldings, and so on. Pieces added after the nailer is up should be attached with finishing nails that can be set and then concealed with a wood dough. Another thought — if applicable — is to use wrought iron nails that have a decorative head.

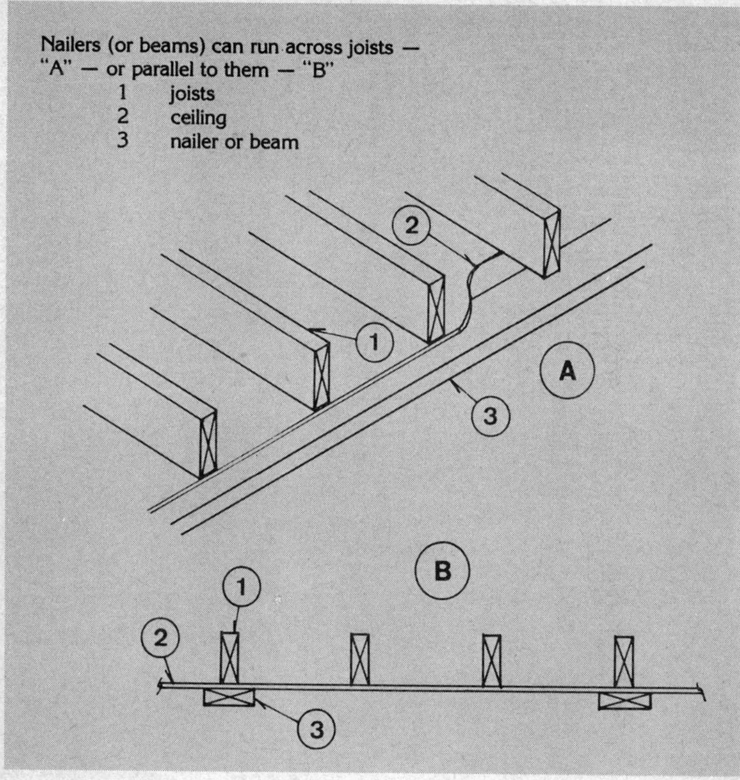


MATERIALS

Almost any wood will be suitable — redwood, cedar, fir, clear or knotty pine; but be sure it's kiln dried. You don't want the new beams to shrink or twist at a later date.

IN GENERAL

Plan before you start. Decide on the number of beams in relation to the size of the room. Beams running the long dimension of the room will tend to make the room look longer. Beams running the short dimension can make the room look wider. Remember that beams tend to lower the ceiling, esthetically and actually. Don't make them so deep that they literally become headaches. You want a minimum of 7½′ between the bottom of the beams and the floor.

## HOW TO ADD CEILING BEAMS (cont'd)

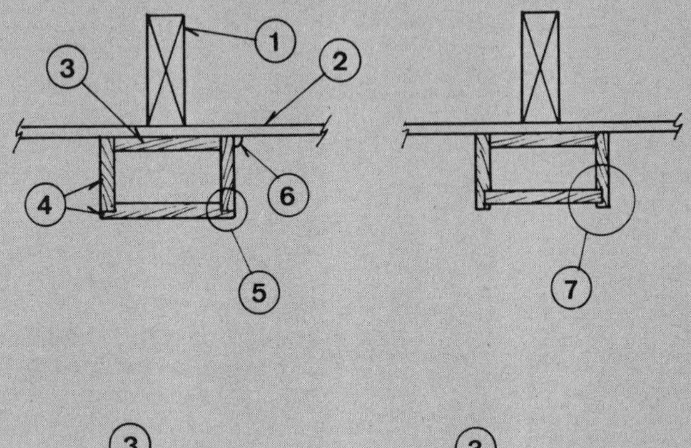


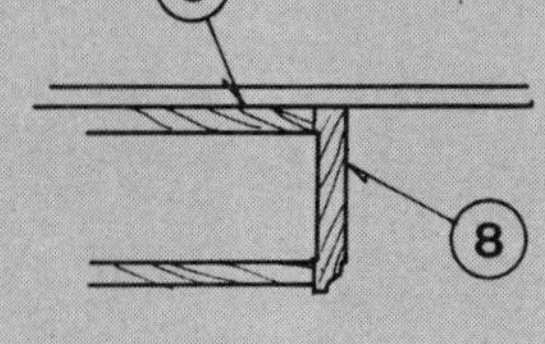


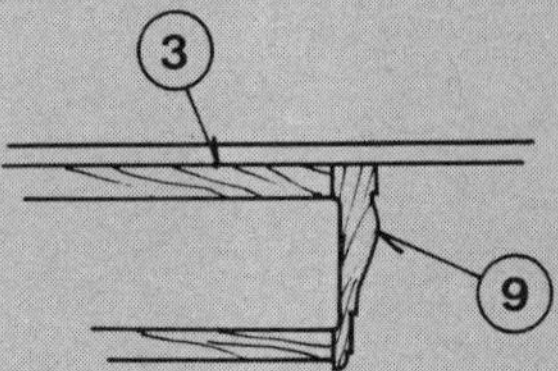


MAKE HOLLOW BEAMS

1 joist
2 ceiling
3 nailer (1x or 2x stock)
4 1x stock for sides and bottom
5 rabbet joint can be used here
6 moulding (optional)
7 Insert the bottom in dadoes for a more modern look.

SIDES CAN BE DONE WITH MOULDINGS

8 baseboard
9 casing

# 5/ BASIC TOOLS AND PRODUCT DATA

Your Georgia-Pacific Registered Building Materials Dealer is the person to see when you purchase your project materials. That shopping trip will go more smoothly if you have a solid, basic knowledge of the goods you'll need. Lumber sizes, grades of plywood, paneling types, etc., are all things you'll need to know about; they're all things we've described in this chapter. Read it over once, then use it for reference later on. You'll have a much better understanding of your own handiwork.

# TOOLS

The tool that will last (almost) forever is a fine bargain even though its initial cost will be more than what's displayed in a take-anything-for-a-dollar bin. Aside from the economics, the good tool helps make you a better craftsperson. For instance, a saw of inferior metal with burred teeth that are incorrectly set will cut wood, but accuracy will be difficult to achieve, and the sawed edge will require much additional attention to make it acceptable.

In all cases, tools added beyond the essential basic assortment we will recommend should be acquired as the need for them arises and only if the need will be a perennial one. There are many tools that fall into the rarely-used category — nice to have but an indulgence if they will merely gather dust. The following suggestions are for the most part in the must-have category.

## BASIC HAND TOOLS

The **crosscut saw** has small teeth with knife-like points. It is designed for cutting across the grain of lumber, but it is also good for sawing all types of plywood. A model that is "taper ground," which usually indicates a quality product, has eight or ten teeth per inch and is 26" long.

**Keyhole** or **compass saws** are different tools, but with much overlap in function. They have narrow blades that taper to a small point and are useful for sawing curved lines and for making internal cutouts; for example, an opening through a panel for an electrical outlet box. A single handle with three different blades is often available as a "nest of saws," one of which can be used to saw metal.

The **backsaw** has teeth like a crosscut saw and has a rectangular blade that is stiffened with a length of steel or brass along its top edge. It's for more precise work than can be accomplished with other saws. For example, it can be used for making the miter cut that is required when two pieces of moulding are joined to make a 90-degree turn. It is often used with a **miter box**, which is simply a guide for accurate cutting.

A 16-ounce **claw hammer** is for general use when driving or pulling out nails. The striking surface should be slightly convex (bell-faced) since this allows you to drive a nail flush without damage to adjacent surfaces. The handle may be hardwood or rubber-sheathed fiberglass or steel. The choice is a personal one. Some old timers say "wood" because it doesn't get cold to the touch in inclement weather. An argument for steel is that it will stay tightly fixed in the head regardless of moisture and changes in temperature.

**Nail sets** are a must because you often drive a finishing nail below the surface of the wood so it can be hidden with wood dough. But a single nail set won't do. Nails come in different sizes, so nail sets are made to match. For the minimum, have sizes 1/32″ and 3/32″.

It's good to have a **flex tape**, but it must be at least an eight-footer since that's the longest dimension of a standard plywood panel. They come in different widths — ¾″ being a good choice even though it is bulkier than others, because it will have the rigidity to span openings without buckling. Markings should include inches and feet and special indications for 16″ on center stud placement. A lock that will hold the tape at any extended position is a good feature.

A **combination square** has many uses. Check corners and cuts for squareness, lay out lines for 45-degree cuts, use it as a depth gauge and as a bench rule. Good ones have a vial built into the head so the tools can be used as a level and a scriber to use as a marker.

A **carpenter's level** should be at least 24″ long and contain three vials so the tool can be used to check both horizontal and vertical planes. Some have a special vial at one end, intended for checking 45-degree angles and slopes.

A **chalk line** is a good idea because it marks long, straight lines. 50′ to 100′ of strong string is encased together with a quantity of chalk dust. Stretch the string tightly between two points, then snap it, and the chalk on the string marks the line. Good ones are refillable with chalk dust and do double duty as a **plumb bob**, useful for marking vertical lines.

There are many types of **utility knives** available, but choose one with replaceable, retractable blades. Its uses are marking cut lines, scoring gypsum board, cutting acoustical tile, and so on.

A **jack plane** should be about 14″ long. There are shorter **bench planes**, but the jack's length helps produce more level edges since it spans across slight bumps you may not see. Use it for smoothing board edges, reducing board widths, removing a smidgen of material so a part will fit just so.

A **block plane** is small enough for one-hand use, so it's especially good for working small pieces of wood. More important, its blade is set at a very acute angle — as slight as 12 degrees — so it can plane end-grain without clogging. Typical use is touching up the bottom or top edge of a door to assure good fit.

**Screwdrivers** we use in the plural because it's important to have a set. Then you can match the driver to the screw with as much torque as necessary without fear of damage to the tool or the fastener. Many sets include one or two drivers with special heads for Phillips-head screws.

A **hand drill** with a set of bits or "points" to form small holes is a must. It works like an eggbeater and will easily drill holes up to about ⅛" diameter. Typical use is drilling "pilot" holes for screws.

An **awl** is also known as the familiar "ice pick." It is useful for marking, especially on metal, and to form starting holes for smaller screws.

**Brace and bits** are for making holes that are larger than those possible with a hand drill. The brace is essentially U-shaped, with a chuck at one end and a flat, knob-type handle at the other. Bits usually range in size from ¼" up to 1", but there are **expansive bits** which are adjustable and permit forming holes as large as 3". Bits used in a brace have screw points so they draw themselves into the wood as they turn. Called bits, they must never be used in a power tool.

**Wood chisels** come in a set, with sizes ranging from ¼" up to at least 1". Good ones cost, but last indefinitely when treated respectfully. Typical applications are forming mortises for door hinges, shaping notches, doing planing jobs when there is no room for the plane.

**Open-end wrenches** also come in a set, with sizes from ¼" to 1". They're not woodworking tools, but you do run into nuts and bolts. Be sure to buy those made of drop-forged steel so they will hold up. Chrome plating will inhibit rust.

**Slip-joint pliers** are made of drop-forged steel and are 8" long. They are called "slip-joint" because the jaws can be adjusted to grip various size objects. They're good to have for general-purpose gripping and bending, even occasional nail pulling. Good ones have a nice pivot action and include a short, sharp section on each jaw so the tool can be used to cut wire.

When buying **sawhorse brackets**, buy two pairs, use them with standard 2 x 4s to make two sawhorses. This way you have supports for a use-anywhere workbench, rests for sawing chores, and legs for a light-duty scaffold. Many brackets are made so legs can be folded for easy storage.

**Clamp-on vise** is the woodworker's type. It is available in different sizes, but don't buy the smallest. Good ones are fitted with hardboard jaw-facings that will not mar what is gripped, and the jaws are replaceable should you damage them. The clamp-on feature allows using the vise anywhere.

There are so many clamps to choose from, but some **C-clamps** make sense in any tool kit. These come in many sizes, but a 3″ pair and a 6″ pair will prove useful. Buy good ones. Those made of welded sheet metal won't hold up. Clamps have a great mechanical advantage, so don't overdo tightening the screw. Protect the work by using small wood pads between the clamp jaws and the wood.

## PORTABLE POWER TOOLS

The **electric drill** is a workhorse because of the many accessories it will drive. Drilling, sanding, buffing, rotary filing, screwdriving, are a few of the many applications that make it a first-choice power tool. But the tool must have the necessary features for the chores to be practical.

You will want double insulation to eliminate the need for grounding; a ⅜″ chuck capacity; a trigger switch-controlled variable speed with a button to lock the switch "on"; an adjustable knob used to maintain a particular speed; a switch so the chuck's rotation can be reversed; a chuck that is lockable with a geared key; and an auxiliary handle useable on either side of the tool's housing when a two-hand grip is advisable.

There's a reason for variable speed — you can suit the rpms to the accessory being used. A reason for the reverse action is that you can remove screws as well as drive them.

The portable **circular saw**, often called a "cut-off" saw, is used for crosscutting, ripping, beveling, mitering, and other routine operations that are done much faster than they can be done with a handsaw. Many models at various prices are available — from about $20 to several hundred — but something in the $50 to $75 range should be a reasonable choice for the average home craftsperson.

Capacity is often judged in terms of blade diameter. This is a logical point at which to start since the larger the blade, the greater the tool's depth of cut. But more important to the average worker is whether the blade will cut through a 2x4 at 45 degrees as well as 90 degrees. Most saws will do this whether they have a 6½″ blade or a 10″ blade. Generally, the larger the blade, the heavier and the more expensive the tool will be. Also, replacement blades will cost more. Why pay for capacity you may never need or tolerate excess weight that can be very tiring?

Do look for double insulation, an easy-to-grip top-side handle with a built-in trigger switch, at least a 1hp motor, and an automatic clutch that lets the blade slip should it jam in a cut. All tools have a spring-loaded blade guard that lifts during a cut and returns to cover the blade when the cut is done. Some models have an electronic brake that stops the blade as soon as the trigger is released.

The portable circular saw can be dangerous if used incorrectly. A common negative occurrence is called "kickback" — the blade binds and tends to travel backwards so the tool moves toward the operator. To avoid it, cut straight, never force the tool, never extend your reach, keep saw blades sharp, and stand so you are not in line with the tool itself.

There are many types of circular saw blades, and it's wise to have an assortment. The one supplied with the tool will be a **combination** blade, good for both crosscutting and ripping lumber. For the best cuts on plywood, choose a special **plywood** blade. A **hollow ground** will leave smooth edges on both lumber and plywood. There are also special **crosscutting** blades and **rip** blades. These should be used when there is much work to be done in either area.

The **saber saw** is excellent for cutting curved lines and for doing internal cutouts, but also good for crosscutting and ripping and other routine work. The blade moves up and down and is gripped only at one end, which is why the tool can work, for example, in the center of a plywood panel without needing a lead-in cut from an edge. There are many types of blades so you can cut metal, ceramic tile, and other materials as well as wood. They are interchangeable and inexpensive enough so they are considered disposable.

A good saber saw will be double insulated, have trigger switch-controlled variable speed (top speed of about 3200 to 3500 strokes per minute), at least a 1/3 hp motor, the capacity to cut through a 2x4, and an adjustable base for bevel cutting.

Some types are called **"scroller" saws**; their design permits the blade itself to be turned. These are very good for getting around a tight corner and for doing scroll-type craftwork.

Check out blades like the **knife-edge**, which is good for cutting materials like leather and linoleum, and the **toothless blade** — its cutting edge is covered with chips of tungsten carbide — for cutting metals and materials like ceramic tile. The tungsten carbide blade can also be used on wood when an exceptionally smooth edge is required, but it will not cut as fast as a conventional toothed blade.

You will want a **finishing sander** (often called a "pad sander") so you don't have to spend hours doing smoothing chores. The tool's motor activates a soft pad over which the abrasive paper is held taut. The pad's action may be reciprocal (to and fro), or orbital (moving in tiny circles), or both. The orbital action, so long as the orbit is small (⅛" or less) and the OPM (orbits per minute) is high (in the 9000 or 10,000 range), will produce the smoothest finishes. The reciprocal action does okay too, but it's best to use with a coarse sandpaper when much material must be removed.

Look for double insulation, ball bearing construction, a direct motor-to-pad drive, a pad in the 3" x 7" range, and clamps that will hold the abrasive paper tautly across the pad. The sandpaper **must** move with the pad. Some tools can be equipped with a lambswool bonnet so they can be used for polishing and buffing as well as sanding.

# LUMBER

## THE PRODUCT

Softwood lumber, the universal building material, is manufactured under strict national rules applying to size, grade, design values, and seasoning. If you know exactly what you want to do with lumber, your description of your project will in most cases enable your building materials dealer to offer you a number of options that will fill the bill. Consult him also about using the lumber you buy, what tools are needed, and how to cut, fasten, and finish for best results. Softwood lumber is available in well over a dozen species, of which Douglas fir and Southern pine, the most plentiful, are also in the strongest category. Other woods include cedar and redwood, both popular for their workability and natural wood beauty. Wood has great strength and is also lightweight and resilient. It is rugged yet easily worked; it is resistant to many acids and does not corrode. No other building material takes and holds paint so well. Wood provides both sound and thermal insulation; it is one of the most efficient insulators of all structural materials.

## GRADES AND TYPES

Those familiar terms — 2x4s, 2x6s, 4x4s, 1x8s — used to designate different sizes of lumber are names rather than actual finished sizes. All western woods and other softwood lumber that move from mills to building sites and to building supply retailers' bins are ordered by these "nominal" sizes. Widths and thicknesses are slimmer than "nominal," as seen in the chart. Most slimming down occurs in the drying-out process and in the planing or finishing. These sizes for seasoned lumber are uniform throughout the country.

| NOMINAL SIZE (in.) | ACTUAL DRY SIZE (in.) |
|---|---|
| 1 x 2 | ¾ x 1½ |
| 1 x 4 | ¾ x 3½ |
| 1 x 6 | ¾ x 5½ |
| 1 x 10 | ¾ x 9¼ |
| 1 x 12 | ¾ x 11¼ |
| 2 x 4 | 1½ x 3½ |
| 2 x 6 | 1½ x 5½ |
| 2 x 10 | 1½ x 9¼ |
| 2 x 12 | 1½ x 11¼ |
| 3 x 6 | 2½ x 5½ |
| 4 x 4 | 3½ x 3½ |
| 4 x 6 | 3½ x 5½ |

## GRADE STAMPS

The function of lumber grade is to provide identification so that the user can purchase wood for the use intended. The official grading agency mark on a piece of lumber is assurance of its assigned grade. Grading practices of these agencies' member mills are supervised to assure uniformity. Shown below is the **(A)** mark for Western Wood Products Association.

**(B)** Each mill is assigned a permanent number for grade stamp purposes.

**(C)** An example of an official grade name abbreviation. The official grade name, as defined by the Association, gives positive identification to grade of lumber.

**(D)** This mark identifies wood species.

**(E)** Symbol denotes moisture content of lumber when unseasoned or "green" lumber. It is recommended that S-Dry lumber be used for all enclosed framing.

## HOW TO BUY

The success of any home improvement begins with using the right lumber grade for the purpose. With the infinite variety of grain color and natural characteristics, wood affords you an individuality unmatched by any other material.

Most building supply home improvement retailers feature extensive lumber departments. Here you will find large assortments of wood products for all types of use. In some centers, lumber is stored or packaged for specific uses in small units for customer convenience.

As you plan your home improvements, remember the best ways to prevent overspending for lumber are: 1) buy the lowest grade of lumber that will do the job; 2) buy the smallest quantity possible.

| | | |
|---|---|---|
| **BOARDS (COMMONS) SIDING PANELING SHELVING SHEATHING AND FORM LUMBER** | No. 1 Common<br>No. 2 Common<br>No. 3 Common | No. 1 Common boards are the ultimate in small-knot material for appearance uses, but less expensive. No. 2 and No. 3 Commons are most often used in housing for paneling, siding, and shelving. Boards are generally available at building material dealers in 1x2 through 1x12. |

**DIMENSION LUMBER / ALL SPECIES**

| | | |
|---|---|---|
| **LIGHT FRAMING** | Construction<br>Standard<br>Utility | This category for use where high strength values are *not* required such as studs, plates, sills, cripples, blocking, etc. |
| **STUDS** | Stud | A popular grade for load- and non-load-bearing walls. Limited to 10′ and shorter. |
| **STRUCTURAL LT. FRAMING JOISTS AND PLANKS** | Select<br>Structural<br>No. 1<br>No. 2<br>No. 3 | These grades fit engineering applications where higher strength is needed, for uses such as trusses, joists, rafters, and general framing. |

# PLYWOOD

### THE PRODUCT

Softwood plywood is a flat panel made of a number of thin sheets of wood (veneer), glued under pressure with the grain of each sheet perpendicular to the grain of the adjacent sheets. This cross-bonding produces great strength in both directions, and the glueline forms a bond that is stronger than the wood itself.

Split-proof and puncture-proof, pound for pound a plywood panel is one of the strongest building materials made. Rigid, stable, and weighing far less than most metals, lumber, or hardboard of equivalent strength, it is easily worked, nailed, glued, and finished. Available everywhere building materials are sold, the most popular plywood panels are 4 x 8 and from ¼″ to ¾″ thick.

### TYPES AND USES

Plywood comes in two basic types, interior and exterior, the principal differences being that more of the lower veneer grades are permitted in the interior type, and the interior glueline does not have to be waterproof. The rule is simple; interior plywood should not be exposed to the weather. Each type is available in a number of appearance grades (A, B, C, D). The veneer used for the face of each panel determines the grade of the product. Unsanded engineered grades are also available for wall and roof sheathing, subfloors, and structural industrial uses.

Plywood is also classified by group based on the strength of the species used to make it. Group I, the strongest, is made up largely of Douglas fir and Southern pine plywood.

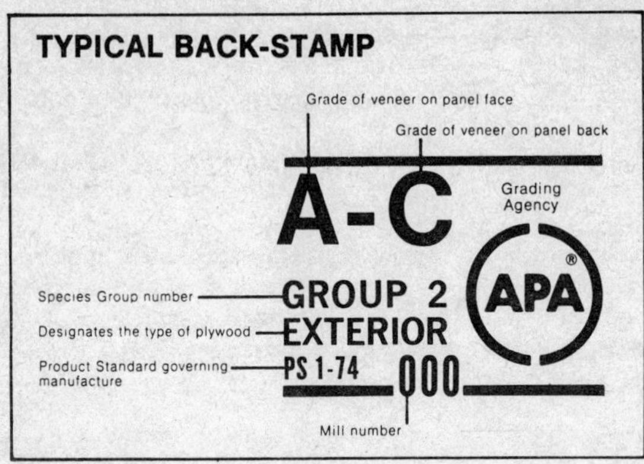


## WHERE TO USE

No building material is as versatile as plywood. Use interior grades for paneling, accent walls, partitions, doors, furniture, cabinets and built-ins, shelving, toys. Use exterior grades for fencing, decking, remodeling. Use engineered grades for wall and roof sheathing, subflooring and underlayment, box beams, utility built-ins, tile backing. There is the right plywood grade for every conceivable building or remodeling job.

## HOW TO BUY AND SPECIFY

There is a tendency to overbuy plywood, most often by substituting exterior for interior grades on the theory that if exterior will stand up to the weather it will do even better indoors. Except where moisture or humidity is present, as in bathrooms and kitchens, this is not true; interior plywood will perform just as well in the controlled environment of the home, and it costs less. Almost all plywood produced in the U.S. is inspected and certified by the American Plywood Association or other certifying agency and bears the agency grade stamp. Plywood is one product you can buy with confidence that it will perform as specified. The most commonly available appearance grades:

**Interior**

**A-D.** For interior applications where the appearance of only one side is important — paneling, built-ins, cabinet shelving.

**B-D.** Utility panel with one smooth, paintable side, for backing, sides of built-ins, utility shelving.

**Decorative B-D.** Rough sawn, brushed, grooved, or striated faces for paneling, accent walls, counter facing, displays.

**Exterior**
**A-C.** For applications where the appearance of only one side is important — siding, soffits, fencing.
**B-C.** Outdoor utility panel with one smooth paintable side.
**Engineered**
**Standard C-D.** The interior unsanded sheathing grade, CDX also available (exterior glue).
**Underlayment.** The interior unsanded grade for underlayment used under resilient floor coverings and carpet. Available with exterior glue.
**Miscellaneous**
**"Shop."** A non-grade stamp plywood panel that is usually marked as "shop." This economical grade may be used for various projects around the home where appearance or structural considerations are not a significant factor.

# PANELING

## THE PRODUCT

Prefinished interior wall paneling is a plywood or processed wood fiber product. The variety of face treatments is almost limitless, but most panelings are designed to bring the natural look of real wood into the home. Many paneling faces are in fact real hardwood or softwood veneers finished to enhance their natural texture, grain, and color. Other faces may be printed, paper overlaid, or otherwise treated to simulate woodgrain.

Paneling is available in a wide spectrum of styles, colors, textures, and price ranges, and there is one suitable for almost any need. With the proper tools, wall paneling is easier to apply than wallpaper, yet is attractive, versatile, and longer lasting.

Panels come in 4′ x 8′ sheets and range in cost from less than five dollars to more than thirty. Factory finishing techniques on both real wood and simulated woodgrain surfaces provide a durable, easily maintained wall.

## TYPES OF FACTORY FINISHED WALL PANELING

### Hardwood and Softwood Plywood

These plywood wall panelings are manufactured with a face, core, and back veneer of a softwood and/or hardwood species. The face and back veneer woodgrains run vertically, with core running horizontally. This gives dimensional strength and stability.

Hardwood and softwood plywood wall paneling is normally ¼″ thick, and some is as thick as 7/16″.

The most elegant plywood panels have real hardwood or softwood face veneers — walnut, birch, elm, oak, cherry, cedar, pine, fir. The subtle variety of texture and grain in real wood panelings makes each one distinctive.

These panels create the rich variety of pattern and warm wood tones only the beauty of nature's own real woods can offer. Georgia-Pacific's Chateau II, Barnplank, Design VIII, and Ol' Savannah are a few of the beautiful real wood face-veneered panelings from which you can select.

**Tropical Hardwood Plywood**

Other plywood panels may have a face veneer of tropical hardwood. Finishing techniques include embossing, antiquing, or color-toning to achieve a woodgrain or decorative look. Panels may also receive a paper overlay, with woodgrain or patterned papers laminated to the face veneer. The panel is then grooved and finished. Many popular panelings like G-P's Gatehouse, Forestflair, and Acry-Tuff are in this category. Most of these panelings are 5/32″ thick.

**Wood Fiber Substrates**

Processed wood fiber (particleboard or hardboard) wall panels are available with grain-printed paper overlays or printed face surface. These prefinished panels are economical yet attractive. Thicknesses available are 5/32″, 3/16″ and ¼″.

Wood fiber substrates, while economically priced and durable, are more subject to moisture conditions, and manufacturer's installation instructions should be followed carefully for cutting, spacing, panel placement, and application by nailing or adhesives.

### Groove Treatment

Most vertical wall panelings are "random grooved" with grooves falling on 16" centers so that nailing over studs will be consistent. A typical random groove pattern may look like this:

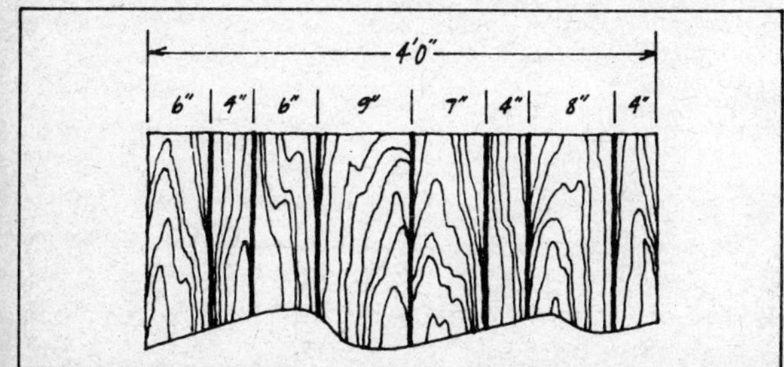


Other groove treatments include uniform spacing (4", 8", 12", or 16") and cross-scored grooves randomly spaced to give a "planked" effect. Grooves are generally striped darker than the panel surface. Grooves are cut or embossed into the panel in V-grooves or channel grooves. Less expensive panels sometimes have a groove "striped" on the surface.

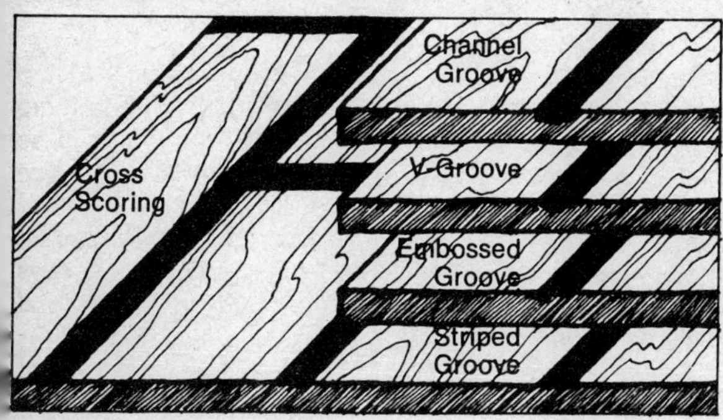


## HOW TO BUY

Paneling, like other products for the home, is available in a wide choice of price categories, from as little as $5 per panel to over $30 per panel. Real wood surface veneered plywood panels are considered "the best." Their price, from about $16 - $35 per 4' x 8' sheet, reflects the quality and beauty of natural hardwood and softwood face veneers. Like fine furniture, real wood panelings are an investment in beauty that will last a lifetime. The warmth and character of real wood adds both value and enjoyment in your home. Fads in wallcoverings come and go, but a lustrous wood surface is always in style.

Generally, you'll find that panelings with a simulated woodgrain finish are less expensive than real wood surfaced panels. Printed or plywood overlaid panelings are excellent choices for many decorating needs and are available for about $9 - $15 per panel. Panelings with a wood fiber substrate fall into the $5 - $8 per sheet category and are good-looking, economical choices for the decorator on a budget.

Whatever your decor or price range, you are sure to find a paneling that's right for you. Beautiful, durable, and versatile, wall paneling is available to suit any decorating taste. Your selection of paneling will take many things into consideration: type of furnishings, room size, number of walls, quantity needed, price, and other preferences. Whatever your final decision, wall paneling will provide years of beauty and easy-to-maintain walls for any room in the home.

# GYPSUM BOARD

## THE PRODUCT

Gypsum board is an engineered building panel consisting of gypsum (hydrated calcium sulfate, a mineral), fibers, and other ingredients, finished on both sides with special paper to provide smooth surfaces and panel reinforcement. Actually a low density rock, gypsum is noncombustible and nontoxic. The properties that make gypsum board an important part of nearly every building in the country are gypsum's inherent resistance to fire and to the transmission of sound.

## CONSTRUCTION ADVANTAGES

Gypsum board walls and ceilings have a number of outstanding advantages:

### Fire Resistance

Gypsum board is an excellent fire barrier, not only because it is noncombustible, but also because it has combined water in the gypsum core. When gypsum is exposed to fire, the water of crystallization is slowly released as steam, and this effectively retards heat transfer.

### Sound Isolation

Excellent sound isolation is obtained by separate framing of the two sides of the wall, fastening the wallboard over a sound control material, such as another gypsum board, and including sound-absorbing materials in the wall cavity.

**Durability**

Gypsum board makes strong high-quality walls and ceilings with good dimensional stability. The surfaces may be easily decorated and refinished during their long life.

**Economy**

Gypsum board products are readily available and relatively easy to apply. They are the least expensive wall surfacing materials available which offer a structurally sound, fire-resistant interior finish.

## WORKING WITH GYPSUM BOARD

Refinishing or installing a new drywall partition or ceiling is not difficult if the job is planned ahead of time. As with any building or remodeling job, first make a sketch of the room to scale. Plan on installing the sheets perpendicular to studs and rafters, and buy your sheets in as long a length as you can conveniently handle, to reduce end joints — which must be staggered if they can't be avoided. Using your sketch, determine the length and number of sheets you need. For ⅜″ and ½″ board use 1⅝″ coated type drywall nails, for ⅝″ board use 1⅞″ nails. Buy 5½ lbs. per 1,000 square feet of board. For each 500 square feet of board you will need three gallons of ready-mix joint compound, and a 250′ roll of wallboard tape.

## WHAT TO BUY

Gypsum board has come to be a specialized product, formulated differently for a growing number of specific end uses. Since it became popular thirty years ago, no other building product with the exception of particleboard approaches gypsum in terms of the research and engineering effort devoted to its development. The types manufactured by Georgia-Pacific include:

**Regular Gypsum Board**

Recommended for single layer application in new construction (½″, ⅝″). Reinforce with G-P joint system products for smoothest face. Use ⅜″ board for application over existing walls.

**Firestop® Gypsum Board**

Develops 45-minute to 3-hour fire resistant ratings depending on wall or ceiling system used. Textile glass filaments and other ingredients keep core intact, even after the chemically combined water has been released.

**Gypsum Sound Deadening Board**

When combined with other gypsum board, this strong, noncombustible ¼″ panel reduces through-the-wall sound transmission.

**Tile Backer Board**

Water resistant designed as a base for the application of ceramic, metal, or plastic tile with adhesives. Asphalt wax emulsion, combined in gypsum core, recommended for bathrooms, kitchens, laundry rooms.

**Insulating Gypsum Board**

Aluminum foil laminated to the back surface provides a continuous vapor barrier on the warm side of the wall. Install with foil side against the studs.

**Gypsum Sheathing**

Core combines asphalt emulsion with gypsum for water resistance. Available 4′ wide square edge for vertical installation and 2′ wide square to T&G edge for horizontal installation.

# HARDBOARD and PARTICLEBOARD

## THE PRODUCTS

Hardboard and particleboard are widely used today for residential construction and do-it-yourself projects. You've probably heard of this type of "man-made" wood product under various descriptions: hardboard and particleboard, pressed wood or board, composition board, fiber board, flakeboard, and other descriptive or brand name product terms.

Essentially, this material is made from wood residue — fiber, chips, flakes, particles, shavings — to produce a usable by-product from the former "waste" material left over in the manufacturing process of lumber and plywood.

While these products are commonly used in industrial applications and in construction, they are finding greater use in projects around the home. It will help you to recognize the different types of hardboard and particleboard and what they are best used for.

## HARDBOARD

Hardboard is a smooth panel without knots or grain, yet it is almost entirely natural wood — cellulose for strength and lignin for bonding power, as in the tree itself. The difference is that the fibers are rearranged to provide special properties. Hardboard is tough and dense. Under most conditions it does not crack, splinter, check, craze, or flake in outdoor environments and is impact resistant. It is generally available in panel sizes up to 4′ wide and 8′ long, in thicknesses from ⅛″ to ¼″.

**Hardboard Types and Uses**

There are three basic types of hardboard:

**Service:** For miscellaneous interior uses such as storage areas, closet liners, shelving, cabinet backs, and drawer bottoms.

**Standard:** For interior paneling, underlayment, screens, and wardrobe doors. Available perforated for storage areas, such as a garage liner where items can be hung from small hooks and brackets inserted in the holes. Special prefinished hardboard decorative panels are also available in a variety of patterns and textures.

**Tempered:** Tempering is a manufacturing process which introduces oil into the board and is permanently "set" with a heat process. This gives the board greater abrasion resistance, strength, and moisture resistance. Used for exterior applications such as soffits, shutters, fencing, flower boxes, windbreakers, and garden sheds.

Other specially treated hardboards are available in exterior siding patterns, both lap and panel.

## PARTICLEBOARD

Particleboard is another engineered wood panel product, consisting of wood residues from lumber and plywood manufacturing operations — mainly planer shavings and veneer clippings — processed and bonded by adding synthetic resins and a wax emulsion for moisture resistance. The result is a highly uniform product noted for its surface smoothness, strong internal bond, good screw and nail holding power, and dimensional stability. Like hardboard it is without knots or grain, but it is less dense and comes in thicker panels.

**Particleboard Types and Uses**

Particleboard may be used for shelving, drawers, bookcases, cabinets, countertops, and the like. Thicknesses generally available are ⅜″ and ½″. It has a very smooth surface as a corestock material, and laminates can be glued easily. It also accepts stain, varnish, paint, or lacquer like any wood product, and for this purpose it can be ordered primed or filled. To minimize warping, finish both sides of each panel identically — critical in applications such as sliding doors.

**Underlayment**

A very widely-used product is ⅝″ 4x8 particleboard underlayment. The standard application is ½″ CDX plywood over floor joists 16″ on center, followed by a second layer of ⅝″ particleboard underlayment. Final layer could be an appropriate carpet and pad. For superior results it is recommended both plywood and particleboard be glue nailed.

## HOW TO BUY AND SPECIFY

Hardboard and particleboard should be specified by intended use, and given the variety of types and thicknesses available, it is best to consult your dealer. Figure your requirements carefully to get the most efficient cuts from standard size panels. Many dealers have cut-to-size capabilities and standard shelving widths and lengths.

# SIDING

## THE PRODUCT

From economical hardboard siding to solid lumber, there's a complete range of siding patterns available to provide the alternative you need to meet any design problem. Plywood sidings come in a wide variety of attractive patterns and textures and combine the natural beauty of wood with the toughness of plywood. Hardboard sidings come in several patterns, and now they are also available with a textured surface. This factory-tempered material is durable, yet easy to work. And, of course, there are a number of types of lumber siding available for that luxurious look.

All sidings are suitable for exterior or interior use. Edge sealing is recommended for all edges on both panel and lap sidings to ensure job performance. Georgia-Pacific sidings are manufactured in accordance with Commercial Standards and association grading rules — and are so identified with a grade stamp. Any product marked "shop," "mill certified," etc., does not meet the applicable standard.

## TYPES OF SIDING

### Plywood

The strength, durability, economy, and ease of installation of plywood make it ideal for exterior siding. That it is attractive is almost a bonus. Virtually all types are available in a variety of patterns and textures in Douglas fir, Southern pine, cedar, and redwood.

**(MDO) Medium Density Overlaid** is a good choice if you want to paint your house. The grade has a smooth, opaque, resin-impregnated fiber overlay fused to the panel face. It accepts the popular water base acrylic house paints beautifully and holds them tenaciously.

**Douglas fir plywood** siding is a good candidate for rustic, stained finishes, and it is virtually indestructible. It is available plain or grooved and comes either rough sawn or smooth.

**Southern pine plywood** has a distinctive grain which also lends itself to paint finishes. It is available either rough sawn, or smooth, plain, or grooved.

**Cedar** is a beautiful wood, and cedar sidings combine that visual appeal with the strength and stability of plywood. It may be stained to emphasize the grain pattern. In addition to the usual patterns and textures, cedar siding is available brushed.

What goes for cedar goes in spades for **redwood plywood** siding, known for its natural beauty and resistance to insects and decay. Available rough sawn or smooth, plain, or grooved.

### Hardboard

The selection of hardboard siding patterns can provide appealing and economical answers to your design problems. They're available smooth or textured with a deeply embossed woodgrain finish. Hardboard is made by bonding wood fibers under heat and pressure to form a tough material that's great for siding. It's dense, smooth, and dimensionally stable. Both lap and panel hardboard sidings come primed or prefinished in a variety of colors.

**Redwood Lumber**

Redwood lumber's natural warmth and beauty make it an excellent material for siding. Sidings are available in several bevelled patterns along with many saw-textured and smooth vertical siding patterns. Plowed fascia is also available, grooved to accept ⅜″ or ¼″ soffit board. It's available natural or primed. Redwood siding needs no further finishing, since it is naturally resistant to insects and decay. It will eventually weather to a silver gray color; however, if additional protection is desired, clear water repellent materials are available. Semi-transparent and heavy-bodied stains may both be used. If paints are used, an oil-based primer should be applied first.

### HOW TO SPECIFY

All plywood panels used for siding are exterior grade plywood manufactured with fully waterproof glue. The most common panel dimensions are 4x8 feet. However, siding panels are also available in 9- and 10-foot lengths. Panel thicknesses vary from ⅜″ to ⅝″ depending on groove depth and span requirements. Look for the grade trademark stamped on the panels when you buy. Almost all plywood produced in this country is inspected and certified by the American Plywood Association or other certifying agency and bears the agency grade stamp — PS 174.

Lumber most often specified as siding is No. 2 and No. 3 Common Board. The official grading agency mark assures uniform quality.

## MOULDINGS

### THE PRODUCT

Unfinished softwood mouldings, mostly pine, fir, cedar, and hemlock, are a precision building product manufactured to national standards as trim material for builders and remodelers. To "trim out" a house means to install and finish the mouldings, the final step in construction. Literally, mouldings are strips of wood ripped from kiln-dried boards up to 16′ in length and milled into about 30 stock patterns, or profiles, continuous throughout their length. Each profile is designed for a primary use, but most have a large number of secondary uses as well.

### TYPES OF MOULDINGS

Standard moulding patterns follow:

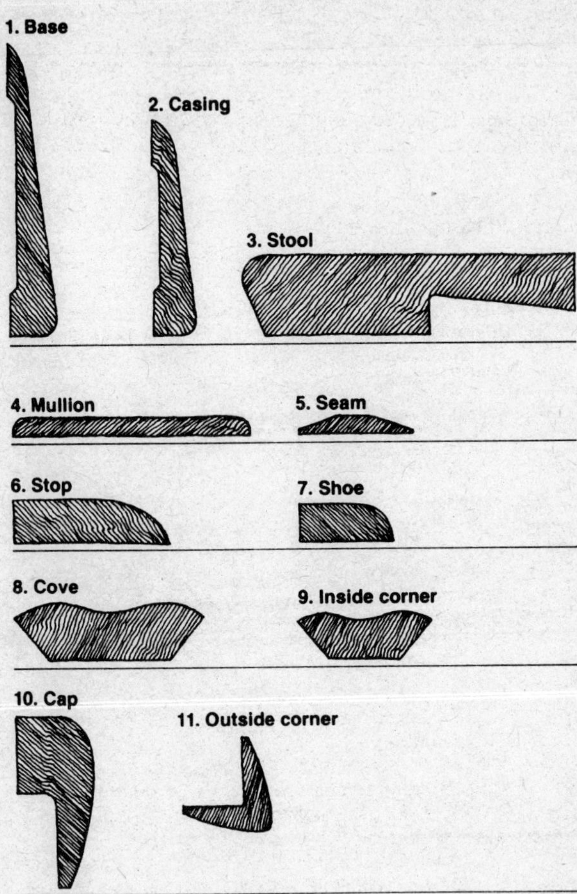


## HOW TO BUY MOULDINGS

Unfinished wood mouldings are available in lengths from 3′ to 16′ and are sold in specified or random lengths — which are less expensive. Order in pieces, pairs, or sets, or on a hundred lineal feet basis (also less expensive). If you intend to paint rather than stain, finger-jointed mouldings are a good buy and are more easily obtained in specified lengths. See your dealer for thickness and width availabilities in the patterns wanted. Bring a scaled sketch with you indicating doors, windows, ceiling type, and wall covering.

# NAILS

## THE PRODUCT

Nails come in many sizes, types, and surface finishes. It is important to use the correct type of nail for your project.

| Joining | Size & Type | Placement |
|---|---|---|
| **Wall Framing:** | | |
| Top plate | 8d common | |
| | 16d common | |
| Header | 8d common | |
| | 16d common | |
| Header to joist | 16d common | |
| Studs | 8d common | |
| | 16d common | |
| **Wall Sheathing:** | | |
| Boards | 8d common | 6″ o.c. |
| Plywood (5/16″, ⅜″, ½″) | 6d common | 6″ o.c. |
| Plywood (⅝″, ¾″) | 8d common | 6″ o.c. |
| **Subflooring** | 8d common | 10″-12″ o.c. |
| **Underlayment** | (1¼″ x 14 ga. | 6″ o.c. edges |
| | annular underlayment nail) | 12″ o.c. face |
| **Roof Sheathing:** | | |
| Boards | 8d common | |
| Plywood (5/16″, ⅜″, ½″) | 6d common | 12″ o.c. and |
| Plywood (⅝″, ¾″) | 8d common | 6″ o.c. edges |
| **Roofing, Asphalt:** | | |
| New construction | ⅞″ through 1½″ galv. roofing | 4 per shingle |
| Re-roofing application | 1¾″ or 2″ galv. roofing | 4 per shingle |
| **Roofing, Wood Shingles:** | | |
| New construction | 3d-4d galv. shingle | 2-3 per shingle |
| Re-roofing application | 5d-6d galv. shingle | 2-3 per shingle |
| **Soffit:** | 6d-8d galv. common | 12″ o.c. max. |
| **Siding:** | | |
| Bevel and lapped | 9d galv. common hot dipped | |
| Drop and shiplap | 8d galv. common hot dipped | |
| Shingles and shakes | 3d-6d galv. shake hot dipped | |
| Plywood, fiberboard, gypsum | 2″ x 14 ga. hot dipped galv. shake | |
| **Doors, Windows, Mouldings:** | 4d-12d casing-finishing | |
| **Furring:** | | |
| Wood strip to masonry | 1½″ or 1¾″ concrete nail | |
| Wood strip to stud or joist | 8d common | |

NOTE: Usage may vary somewhat due to regional differences and preferences.

| Joining | Size & Type | Placement |
|---|---|---|
| **Paneling:** | | |
| Wood | 4d-8d casing-finishing | 24″ o.c. |
| Hardboard | 2″ x 16 ga. annular | 8″ o.c. |
| Plywood | 3d casing-finishing | 8″ o.c. |
| Gypsum | 1¼″ annular drywall | 6″ o.c. |
| **Lathing:** | 4d common blued | 4″ o.c. |

**Sizes**

Nail sizes start at 2d which is 1″ long. They range up to 60d which is 6″ in length. The 2d through 10d are in ¼″ increments, i.e. — a 2d is 1″ long; 3d is 1¼″, etc. Nails above 16d increase by ½″ increments.

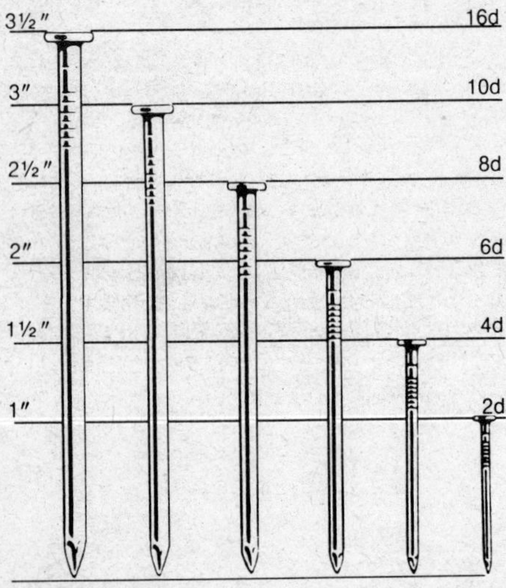


**Surface Finishes**

**Bright:**

After manufacture, nails are tumbled to remove dirt and "chips," and packed uncoated.

**Galvanized:**

A zinc coating is applied, via either hot-tumbler method or electrolysis to protect against atmospheric corrosion.

**Cement-Coated:**

An adhesive is applied via tumbler to provide increased holding power.

**Blued:**

Nails are sterilized by heating them until an oxidation layer is formed.

# HOW TO FIGURE YOUR PROJECT

If you are an accomplished handyman with scores of projects to your credit, you'll probably find this chapter contains tips you've already discovered for yourself. On the other hand, if your handyman experience has been limited to an occasional weekend project, then here are a few fundamental suggestions that can save you time and money as you size up your project and select the right materials to do the job.

Laying out your project on graph paper is the first step. A scaled drawing will enable you to measure with reasonable accuracy and to visualize the completed design. Don't worry about the quality of your draftsmanship. Any rough sketch will do as long as it contains accurate measurements. The simplest layout can be an important means of communication — for yourself as you think through the project and for your building materials dealer when you order the supplies you need. For example, here's how a rough sketch (drawn on the graph paper) can be used to figure the number of panels needed to panel a room. First, it's necessary to determine the room's perimeter. This is merely the total of the widths of each wall in the room. Then, use the conversion table below to determine the number of panels needed for your project.

| Perimeter | No. of 4'x8' Panels Needed |
|---|---|
| 36' | 9 |
| 40' | 10 |
| 44' | 11 |
| 48' | 12 |
| 52' | 13 |
| 56' | 14 |
| 60' | 15 |
| 64' | 16 |
| 68' | 17 |
| 72' | 18 |
| 92' | 23 |

As an example, if your room walls measured 14'x14' x 16'x16', this would qual 60' or 15 panels required. To allow for areas such as windows, doors, eplaces, etc., use the following deductions:

**Deductions**

| | |
|---|---|
| Door | ½ Panel (A) |
| Window | ¼ Panel (B) |
| Fireplace | ½ Panel (C) |

Thus, the actual number of panels for this room would be 13 pieces (15 pieces minus 2 total deductions). If the perimeter of the room falls between the figures in the above table, use the next highest number to determine the panels required. These figures are for rooms with an 8′ ceiling or less.

Your building materials dealer is ready and willing to assist you in any way he can to make your project a success. He can take a look at your rough sketches and help you determine the exact type and quantities of materials you'll need. But there are some things you can do to help your dealer help you. First, shop during the week if you can. If you have a big project, or need a lot of technical assistance, you'll probably get better help on weekdays. During the week your dealer has time to review your plans and help you pick the right lumber at the right price. Bring your plans with you when you go shopping. In fact, you can never bring too much information with you. Write down everything about your project or material needs. And always make all your measurements before coming to the lumber store. Whether your project is a new kitchen cabinet or building bookshelves, be sure to measure the area accurately. Armed with your drawings and dimensions, tell the salesman where your project is going to go. The more information you can supply, the greater the chances that you'll leave with the right sizes. When you make up a materials list, it should be as detailed as possible. For example, if your project calls for 12 pieces of 2x4 exactly 8 feet long, list the item that way. Don't add them up to make it 96 feet of 2x4 because the supplier might include a few pieces only 6 feet long. When he fills your correctly-stated order, he may give you 6 pieces 16 feet long, but cut to your needs.

When you order lumber, remember there is an accepted way to state your order. If you follow these specifications you'll avoid many of the slip-ups that can occur. First: state the number of pieces needed. Second: the size of lumber you need, in thickness, width, and length. And last: the grade and species. For example: "Ten pieces, 1x12 eight feet long, No. 2 common white pine."

One way to keep your lumber costs down is to order the smallest quantity needed. To buy only as much as you need, plan carefully. If you design a bookcase with 10-inch wide shelves, a 1x10 board (9½ inches wide) won't work. You'll have to buy a 1x12, trim it back and throw the waste away. It's even more important to design to standard lengths. (Sawmills usually produce lumber in lengths from 4 to 20 feet in multiples of 2 feet.) If you plan an 8′6″ long bookcase for your den, you may be able to buy 9-foot boards and only lose 6 inches on each, but more than likely you'll end up with 10-foot boards and trim 18 inches of waste. That's expensive scrap. Whenever possible, design all projects in multiples of 2 feet.

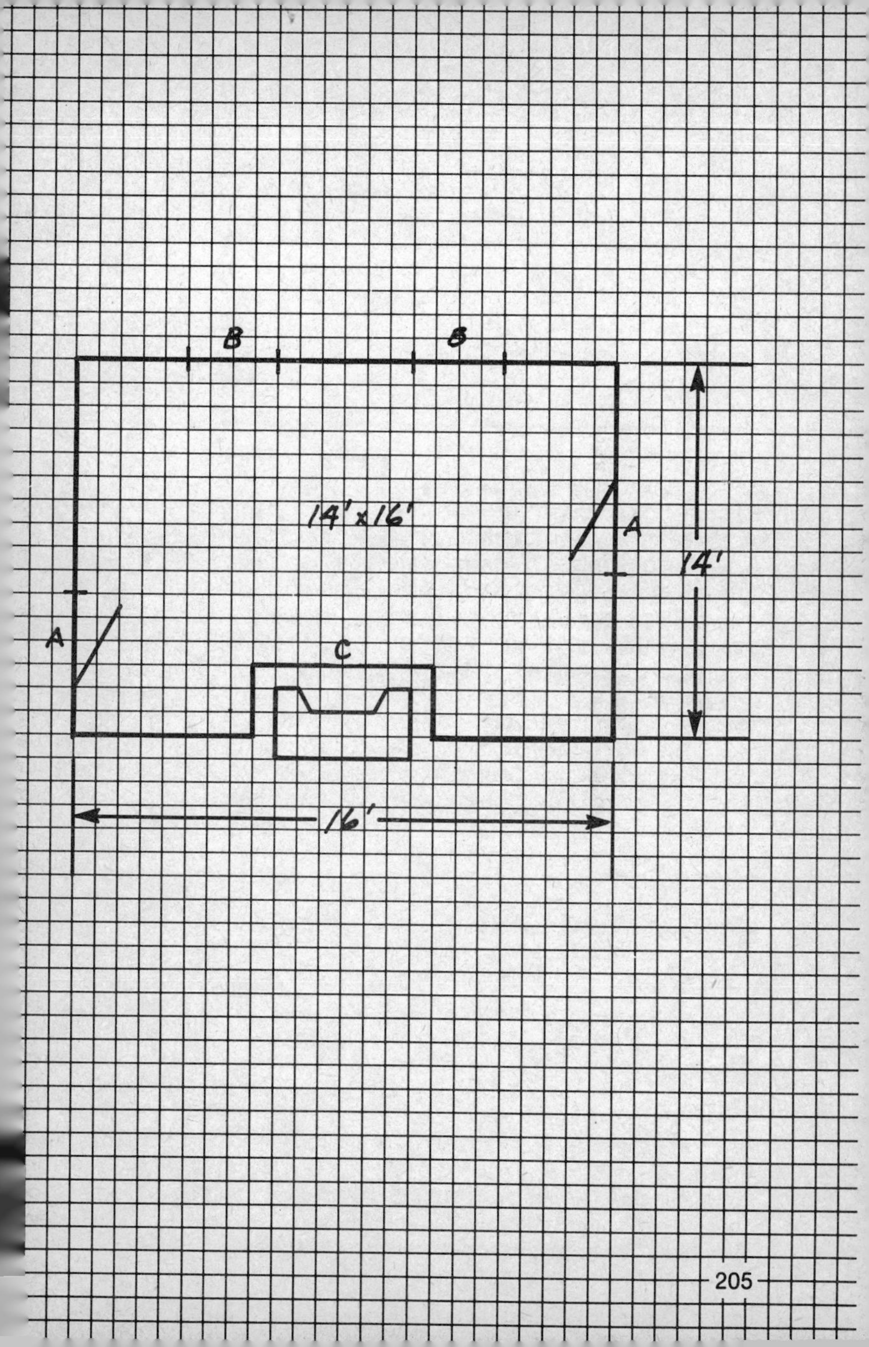

B
B
14'x16'
A
14'
A
C
16'

# GEORGIA-PACIFIC LITERATURE

For additional ideas or help with your remodeling or decorating projects, send for any of the following Georgia-Pacific literature:

1. How to Install Wall Paneling
2. The Designer's Touch for Living Rooms
3. The Designer's Touch for Kitchens and Dining Rooms
4. The Designer's Touch for Family Rooms
5. The Designer's Touch for Bedrooms
6. Do-it-Yourself Gypsum Board Application Instructions
7. Do-it-Yourself Gypsum Wall and Ceiling Texturing
8. Do-it-Yourself Gypsum Wall Repairing and Patching
9. Redwood Fence Ideas
10. Redwood Deck Ideas
11. Paneling Catalog
12. How to Make Beautiful Things Happen with Walls

---

Send to: **Georgia-Pacific, 900 S.W. 5th Ave., Portland, Oregon 97204**
Attn: Advertising Department

Please send me the literature items circled.

1 2 3 4 5 6 7 8 9 10 11 12

Name ____________________________________

Address ____________________________________

City ____________________ State __________ Zip ______

# HOW TO ORDER PROJECT PLANS

Enter project plan number on order form as indicated.
Each plan costs $2.50.

| Plan | Page |
| --- | --- |
| 101 | 130 |
| 102 | 132 |
| 103 | 136 |
| 104 | 140 |
| 105 | 144 |
| 106 | 146 |
| 107 | 149 |
| 108 | 152 |
| 109 | 154 |
| 110 | 156 |

---

Mail to: **Project Plans**
Hudson Home Publications, 289 S. San Antonio Rd., Los Altos, Calif. 94022

Please send me Plan No. ________ ; Cost $ ____________________

Postage and Handling (35¢ each) ....... $ ____________________

California residents add 6% sales tax .... $ ____________________

TOTAL $ ____________________

Allow 10 working days for delivery

Name (print) ______________________________________

Address ______________________________________

City ____________________ State ____________ Zip ____________

Phone ( ) ______ - ____________

**Make Check or Money Order Payable to Hudson Home Publications / GP1**

(Sorry, no C.O.D.'s)